COMPARATIVE RELIGION

COMPARATIVE RELIGION

A.S. GEDEN

GYAN

Published by

Gyan Publishing House
5, Ansari Road
Daryaganj, New Delhi-110002
Phone: 011-47034999, 9811692060
E-mail: books@gyanbooks.com

Distribution Network
gyanbooks.com
India, USA, Canada, UK, Australia, France

ISBN : 978-81-212-3267-8 (PB)
First Published, London, 1922

2nd Impression 2020

Printed at: Gyan Press, Delhi.

Comparative Religion
Author: A.S. Geden

PREFACE TO THE FIRST EDITION

THE following work is and can only be a brief introduction to a serious and most important subject. For those whose interest is enchained, and who desire to pursue it further, it is hoped that the bibliography at the end of the book will afford aid and guidance for more unrestricted study. Only a selection from a great and growing literature has been possible. In this respect, as in many others, the *Encyclopædia of Religion and Ethics*, edited by Dr. Hastings, is a treasury of all good things. There are many ways, however, of approaching the study of Comparative Religion. The best, in the judgement of the writer, is that of attempting to gain an insight into the teaching of some of the more influential religions of the world, collating then the results obtained, and estimating the significance of truths held in common and of the cleavages and differences which profoundly separate them. It is from this point of view that the following introduction has been written. If it may conduce in some measure to a deepened interest in a subject that yields to none in urgency and promise, the purpose and hope of the writer will have been fulfilled.

A. S GEDEN.

Egham,

February, 1917

PREFACE TO THE SECOND EDITION

THE need for a second edition has given me the opportunity of adding the titles of two or three recent works of importance to the Bibliography, and of making a few minor corrections and amplifications in the text. In all essentials, however, the latter is not altered. Of noteworthy publications also in this, as in other sciences, the number has been inconsiderable. The events of the last five years, however, have accentuated the need for the service which in my judgement the science of Comparative Religion is able to render in the furtherance of mutual understanding and sympathy, of harmony of religious outlook and aims, and of a realisation of the supreme importance of the fundamental principles which underlie all real and sincere worship and religious endeavour. A sympathetic knowledge of the thoughts and ideals of other peoples will be more effective than anything else to promote the unity of the faith, though it will never sustain a unity of form, or an impracticable sameness of expression. If the brotherhood of the spirit can be established, there will be no further clash of material arms. In this field the workers are all too few. I can only renew the hope and wish that through this little book some may gain a broader, richer apprehension of the good and beautiful in the lives and hearts of men.

A. S. GEDEN.

Harpenden,
September, 1921.

CONTENTS

COMPARATIVE RELIGION

PART I

AN INTRODUCTION AND A SURVEY

WITHIN a comparatively short period of time the science of Comparative Religion, or, as some prefer to term it, the "Comparative Study of Religions," has gained a high, perhaps the highest place among the sciences. To the pursuit and elucidation of this new science many scholars in many countries have devoted their energies. It is right that it should be so; for in a very real sense religion with all that it implies and prescribes is the highest interest of mankind. It has been reasonably maintained that from a religious source scientific, as well as philosophic thought has its beginnings. Whether this be true or not—and the discussion is of little more than academic interest—the modern science is far from being a matter of concern to the scholar alone, if the latter term be understood in the narrower sense of a man withdrawn from the rough and immediate contact with the world, and possessing his soul in quietness and study. Rather is it the most immediate and important interest of all, from the refined and abstract thinker to the practical student and man of the world. In proportion as the mind is greater than the body, and the mental and spiritual qualities more decisive of all grave issues than the bodily, the sciences that deal with the faculties of the mind and soul will be more fundamental than those which contribute only to material aims. The former are often regarded as more open to controversy, to differences of judgement and interpretation, and as less amenable to strict proof. The assumption is not strictly correct or justifiable; a precisely contrary assertion has been made and maintained on not unreasonable or unintelligible grounds. The importance of both, to men doubly constituted of mind and body, is beyond question.

Least of all can the teacher, whose duty it is to instruct, guide and inform others, afford to neglect the study of Comparative Religion. To him there can be nothing more significant than the religious movements of human thought in their development and expression in history, inadequate and inarticulate as these may often have been, yet containing the promise of the more complete and satisfying forms in which they present themselves in our own day. To those who endeavour to study the present in the light of the past, the latter is not a disconnected and isolated whole, but a real link in a continuous progress, which has suffered many set-backs, but has never really lost sight of its high aim. The science of Comparative Religion has its part to play in the general advance, to vindicate and sustain intellectual freedom, and to aid men to realise that there are moral and spiritual issues above the material and the visible, of which these last can at their best give but a faint premonition.

IMPORTANCE OF THE SCIENCE

It may be thought that the claim to pre-eminent importance thus asserted in the name of Comparative Religion can with difficulty if at all be justified either by the services it has rendered to mankind, or by its present or prospective success in solving the riddles and alleviating the doubts that beset the human mind as it faces the unknown future. The path of material science or even of philosophy, if strewn with failures, is rendered glorious also by achievement. Can the science of Comparative Religion point to any similar record of substantial accomplishment in support of its claim to a hearing? If criticism of this character is to any extent justified, the youthfulness of the science may well be urged in defence, and its rapid growth from a position of almost complete obscurity to one that commands the attention of many of the foremost men of our time in the world of literature and thought. That even so it has not failed to contribute practically and usefully to the sum of human knowledge the following pages may hope to show. That its promise for the future is great, no one who has studied it even superficially would deny. It makes no pretension to be prophetic, either of the precise direction its researches will take, or the issues to which they will lead. Its best students are too fully conscious of the difficulties in their path to be confident of the lines of its future course, or disposed to celebrate beforehand the brilliancy of its coming conquests. Perhaps its best recommendation is that it endeavours to gather and assimilate truth from all sides, to winnow the chaff from the wheat, and to follow the truth thus found wherever it may lead. Meanwhile it assumes as its province all human thought that in however remote a degree may rightly be described as religious, together with all acts and observances in which such thought finds or has found expression. Religious instincts and conceptions, the impulses that lead to religious observance or system, however inchoate the latter may be, together with all that is involved therein, historical or actual or affording reasonable inference as to the future, are claimed to lie within its sphere.

Human Nature Religious

It is generally agreed that man is essentially religious in his aptitudes and aims. Deeply engrained within his nature is some conception, rudimentary and ill-defined though it may be, of a power or powers external to and independent of himself, to which he is under obligation, and with which he more or less of necessity enters into relations. In regard to this, hasty and ill-considered assertions have not infrequently been made in the past by travellers and others who were insufficiently in sympathy with the peoples they described. For the most part these assertions were founded upon misunderstanding. It is most difficult, perhaps almost impossible, for the foreigner without long and intimate acquaintance to arrive at a just comprehension of the real convictions and beliefs of the tribes with which he comes into contact. In all that concerns their most profound and cherished beliefs they are exceedingly reticent, and like children will often make pretence with intent to deceive, partly also through fear of incurring ridicule. Not a few instances have occurred of reports received even from those who have sojourned among them for some considerable time, of peoples supposed to be definitely atheist, without any conception of a god or higher power. Further investigation has always proved that such statements were made under a misapprehension, which was not always free from bias. When communication through an interpreter, whose knowledge is very likely to be in inverse proportion to his zeal, is added to the other possibilities of mistake, the difficulties of arriving at a just and secure conclusion are greatly enhanced. Wherever a real and patient investigation into savage or primitive beliefs has been practicable, the reports in question have proved to be unfounded. No tribe or people exists, or as far as we know has ever existed, to whose mind there has not been present the more or less vague conception of a power beside and beyond themselves, which we may call if we will a god. It is perhaps doubtful whether individual men of any nationality have ever been genuinely atheistic in belief. Uncompromising profession of atheism is sufficiently common; and for the purposes of ordinary life this may be taken at its face value, and is undoubtedly often honest and sincere. It is certain, however, that no clan or tribe collectively has been without a dim realisation of the supernatural, perhaps more accurately of extra-natural powers, to which they paid the homage of a collective recognition and regard.

Animism

To assert that these powers were in the first instance in any way conceived as personal would be to go beyond the evidence. The contrary is probably true—that the early thought of man did not make the attempt to frame any idea of personality with regard to the nature or interpretation of the external universe. The late Census Commissioner and Home Secretary to the Government of India, Mr. H. H. Risley, made some very just remarks on this subject in his Report on the Indian Census of 1901, which though they have been quoted more than once may well be repeated here: "It (*i.e.*, animism) conceives of man as passing through life surrounded by a ghostly company of powers, elements, tendencies, mostly impersonal in their character, shapeless phantasms of which no image can be made and no definite idea can be formed. Some of these have departments or spheres of influence of their own: one presides over cholera, another over smallpox, another over cattle disease; some dwell in rocks, others haunt trees, others again are associated with rivers, whirlpools, waterfalls, or with strange pools hidden in the depths of the hills. All of them require to be diligently propitiated by reason of the ills which proceed from them"; that is to say, an indefinite number of vague impersonal forces, rather than a personal and effective will, present themselves to the consciousness of primitive man; and upon these he bases his desires and fears with regard to the unseen.

Comparative Religion therefore at the outset has to

deal with these inchoate forms of religious life, to estimate their value, and to endeavour to trace thei various ramifications and to arrange and classify the modes in which they exhibit themselves. Perhaps it is hardly exact to designate them as "religious" in any real sense of the term, so uncertain and elusive are they. But if an unbroken line of development can be followed from the first beginnings, the unconscious dawn of a faith in the unseen, to the highest convictions and postulates of the great religions of the world, the comparative science will be justified in taking account of the ultimate origins. In one sense no doubt these beliefs, however elementary or universal they may be, are not yet "religion." A mere assurance or conviction, even though it concerns a region unknown and external to the man himself, is not necessarily or even probably religious; and it will depend in part upon the definition that is given to the term in question how far these beliefs may rightly claim to be so designated. It would not be difficult to define "religion," and to limit its content, in terms which would exclude ideas of this nature. In so doing, however, much more would be set aside, to which by general consent the name of "religion" or "religious" belief would not be refused. It is preferable, if that can be done, to allow the term to define itself by trial and experience, in a broad and comprehensive manner, rather than to hedge it about with exceptions and restrictions, which not improbably may prove too abstract and complex to hold good of man in general seeking contact with the unseen and the supernatural.

Definition

It is admittedly difficult to present a satisfactory definition of "religion"; nor is the problem rendered any more easy by the fact that most men think they know what it is. Of the definitions that have been suggested or offered not a few have been self-condemned by their length and obscurity. Yet it is necessary to attempt to gain some conception of what is implied in the word, to reduce to its simplest terms that which in its larger acceptation seems to most men to imply so much, and which means something to us all. Undoubtedly religion is more than belief, or belief accompanied by observances of a stated kind or directed to a stated end. If it is added that the belief must be of or in external powers, whether impersonal or personal, not much real progress has been made. It would seem that the attitude of mind of the man himself is involved to a larger extent than has sometimes been allowed. An abstract or indifferent conviction or belief would not be religion. If, however, to the belief you add the assurance that it is not only desirable but possible to enter into immediate relations with the unseen and intangible powers of the world around, you come very near to a religious faith. Primitive man appears to have made the attempt to establish such relations in two different ways. On the one hand, he has sought to compel them to lend him their aid, and to place their strength and resources at his disposal, in order that he may secure some end or object which appears to him desirable; or on the other hand, he has endeavoured to propitiate them, to present an offering or to render them their supposed due, that their wrath may be appeased, and they may be induced to regard the giver favourably in the practical manner of return benefits. The former of these is the way of magic, the latter of religion; the wizard endeavours to constrain the unearthly powers, the priest to turn away their anger and to secure their good-will. And the question often raised, and sometimes too hastily and dogmatically answered, whether religious belief is an immediate product and descendant of magic or *vice versa*, does not admit of a direct affirmative or negative reply. In some instances a connection by descent may be established, but this will be rare and will not involve the extinction either of the one or the other tendency. More often each will pursue its own course of development within its own sphere, and only in the higher reaches of thought and experience will religion place an effective check upon magical conviction and practice.

Worship

The simplest terms therefore in which to define religion and to distinguish it from magic, with which in reality it has little to do, are probably those of *worship*. The attitude which man adopts towards the powers above and around him is instinctively that of awe and reverence. They are greater and stronger than he, more unaccountable in their activities, more potent in their effects. Science will eventually teach him to understand and to control them; but for primitive man science has no existence or meaning, except in the form of the pseudo-science of magic. And if it be objected that worship, however crude and self-seeking it may be, implies a personal object of regard, to whom the worship is presented, the answer appears to be that in actual practice and in the earliest movements of religious thought this is not so. The intangible impersonal force which stirs in the wind, resides in the grove, or manifests itself irresistibly in the tempest, is not to the mind of primitive man a person in any real sense of the word. It is not sufficiently definite or individualised to be conceived in personal terms. Nevertheless he endeavours to propitiate it with gift and prayer, if it is unkindly malignant or hostile, or presents a thank-offering if he has experienced through its agency some good or hopes to move it to generosity and beneficence in the present or future occasions of need.

THE ORIGINS

Many students of Comparative Religion appear to have assumed as an axiom that by investigation of the beliefs of existing savage tribes it would be practicable to ascertain the beginnings of religion itself; that difficult as the task might prove to be, if the convictions and faith that inspired the most primitive religious customs and practices of peoples living on the lowest grade of savage life could be probed to the very utmost, the issue would reveal to us the beginnings of religious thought, the origins from which have grown up the manifold and rich developments of the present. It is manifest, however, that these primitive beliefs, rudimentarv and elemental as they undoubtedly are, are yet at a far remove from an absolute beginning. They represent a stage which, measured by centuries of change and progress, is perhaps as distant from the starting-point as the complex and highly developed existing systems of religion are from them. Of that earlier and prolonged condition which antedates what we call primitive belief we know nothing. To term such beliefs primitive is, indeed, in one sense to beg the question. They are demonstrably not primitive, if by this word we intend to imply that nothing preceded them or formed the basis and antecedent condition upon which they have been built up, and by which they have been formally determined. They have advanced considerably beyond the starting-point; but of the direction and extent of the progress made we are necessarily and inevitably ignorant. Tentative and reasonable conjecture may illuminate the way backward, but it can never attain to the certainty of ascertained truth.

It is in itself improbable also that of so complex and far-reaching a subject as religious belief and observance, with regard to which men feel that their highest interests are involved, any one single source or cause should be predicable, to the exclusion of others. Natural development and the variety of human instincts and passions would seem to suggest the contrary. Much ingenuity and research however have been expended on the attempt to trace all back to one primary cause or origin, but without success; and among those who have made the attempt, scholars in many instances of acknowledged reputation and learning, there is no general agreement as to the definition or character of the unique source assumed. The results attained or asserted by one have not been universally or without question accepted by others. The variety and discrepancy of the results is itself evidence of the intricacy of the problem. The failure therefore of all such attempts in the present state of our knowledge, attractive as they undoubtedly are, must be confessed. The origins of religion are not simple, and cannot be stated in terms of a singular conception. It does not follow however that if we were in possession of larger insight and more complete data these complex beginnings, which in reality are not beginnings but stations or stages in a long process of development, might not be resolved or led back to a primary elemental source, to which they all owe their initial impulse and inspiration.

Genealogical Relations

These primitive beliefs and practices again are at a far remove from the highly organised cults and elaborate creeds of the more civilised and thoughtful peoples of the present time. It is worth while to emphasize once more that Comparative Religion is concerned with both, and endeavours to institute comparisons and to draw inferences of value from all sides, from the earliest ascertainable movements of religious thought, striving to find for itself modes of expression, to the most highly developed and complex forms and systems that have been evolved in the course of the centuries. Between these there exist or have existed an infinite number of varieties of intermediate beliefs. It is safe to assert that there has been no absolute break or hiatus; that the lower has moved forward by an orderly progress into the higher, that the higher in practically all instances retains traces of its lowly source or origin. The movement has not always been in a forward or upward direction. There have been instances of retrogression and degradation, the processes of mental and spiritual decay operating upon an entire people, as they are seen to do upon an individual. How far such instances may be assumed to be exceptional, whether or to what extent they may be regarded as periodical or due to a more or less rare combination of circumstances is a much disputed question. It is manifest that on a broad view of the issue the advance made and the ground gained have been more than considerable. Moreover, the tribes and peoples of mankind are not isolated and destitute of opportunity and capacity for mutual intercourse and the exchange of ideas; and as far as our knowledge of the constitution of human society and life extends, these conditions have in general always and everywhere existed and been utilised. The hypothesis of a primitive human race existing in absolutely self-contained and separate units or families, without acquaintance and never in touch with one another, is a pure assumption destitute of any real ground or support.

Were our knowledge therefore adequate and sufficiently extensive, to every religious opinion or system might be assigned its place on the wide-spreading genealogical tree of human thought, wherein no branch is disconnected with the rest of the branches and with the trunk. And as the languages of mankind, numerous and diverse as they are, are for the most part at least traceable back ultimately to a primary form or origin, to which they are indebted for their birth and being, so it is with religious speculation and thought. In neither case of course are the data at our disposal which would enable us to reconstruct the genealogy in its entirety. Perhaps they are more deficient and irrecoverable for religion than for language. The conclusion however is certain, that the various religious systems of the world, distant and mutually diverse in principle and practice as they may appear, are not so many independent inventions, but are interconnected, each of them with a long and reasonable history.

We must therefore be content to deal with the evidence to hand, to classify and arrange, and to draw such conclusions as the facts before us appear legitimately to warrant. If there is a sphere and place for conjecture, it will be narrow and limited in its scope, and will take the form in general of an endeavour to follow up lines of thought and inference suggested by the religious conceptions and practices which are certified by other and more sure methods of research. Whether such conjecture, essaying to throw light on the primary and fundamental origins of religious faith, will ever be able to trace back existing modes of observance and forms of belief to a single all-comprehending source, is very doubtful. It is however one of the problems to which the science of Comparative Religion may reasonably address itself, even if a final and certain conclusion is beyond reach. Do the many and varied streams of human belief and action which may be regarded as more or less definitely religious flow from one and the same head-waters? Are the almost infinitely diverse forms that have developed or been promulgated in the course of the centuries reducible to one primary form or source? Or to state the problem otherwise, did all men in the infancy of belief experience the same promptings to worship, moved by the same impulses, and giving expression to the same rudimentary convictions and ideas? The question, if it be regarded as implying and including an enquiry as to the nature of the supposed unique source, is ultimately no doubt unanswerable. The materials for a definite and final conclusion are wanting. There are indications however which would suggest an answer in the affirmative, although it may be impossible in the nature of things to support the inference by definite and conclusive evidence. The rich variety of present-day system and cult is based on certain fundamental conceptions, which are not entirely unrelated, and which therefore, even if we cannot trace the steps, it is not unreasonable to conclude do go back to a common ancestor or beginning. Analogy, however, and conjecture are responsible for the inference; and there have been great differences of opinion as to the character of the assumed source.

Inferences from Primitive Races

Accordingly an enquiry into the origins of religion, such as a true science of Comparative Religion must presuppose and upon which it depends, assumes as its basis research into the beliefs and practices of tribes and individuals, whom it is usual to call primitive. By which term is meant that living apart from all contact with the ideals and ways of civilisation, and uninfluenced by the teaching or example of a higher type of the human race, they occupy the earliest stage or degree on the path of progress of religious thought that can come within our direct cognisance. They are at many removes, how distant we are unable to determine, from the actual beginning. There is, moreover, in their case this inestimable advantage over all methods of theorising or conjecture, that we are able to make direct observations and inquiries, and to revise and check conclusions. Mistakes may be corrected and wrong inferences set aside or modified by reference to the peoples themselves, as long as they exist. The evidence may be tested and revised as often as is necessary, and needs only careful and accurate interpretation to render it entirely reliable. It is obviously of the utmost importance to secure a record of all such primitive beliefs in the fullest possible form, while there is time and opportunity. The observation and experience of travellers and scientific expeditions during the past years have accumulated a store of material of the greatest value, which forms a secure foundation for theory and conclusion. In view of the rapidly changing conditions of savage life, and the comparatively few tribes whose beliefs and customs remain unmodified by contact with the influences of a more advanced culture and civilisation, it is most important that no opportunity of registering the creed and habit of primitive or natural man should be lost.

From Ancient Peoples

A further but much inferior source of information with regard to the origins of religious faith is to be found in the records of ancient peoples and civilisations. These are ready to our hand in their ancient literature, and may be deciphered on their monuments and tombs, and to a less extent are recoverable from the living traditions of their descendants. Upon all of these it is worth while to draw, and they contribute not unimportant elements to the formation of a just and complete picture of primitive religion. In some instances they carry us back for thousands of years; and always in the nature of the case they are earlier in time than evidence acquired from contemporary tribes and peoples. It might be argued therefore that on the ground of antiquity alone they bear testimony to a stage or stages of belief nearer to the primitive source, and approximating more closely to the earliest form which religious faith and worship assumed, when they both began to be. It is only however to a very limited extent that this conclusion appears to be justified. Successive strata of belief and practice are not generally coincident with stages of progress as measured by the centuries. At one time and in one direction the advance will be more rapid, at another it lags behind. Moreover, it is for the most part the more highly cultured and civilised peoples who have left us these records; and they are patently not less but more advanced in all that pertains to the higher regions of reflective ideas and thought than the savage tribes of our own day. Almost the sole evidence of the religious practices and faith of the earlier historical and pre-historical periods is to be found in the ancient tombs and cemeteries of Egypt and other countries. Such evidence at the best is scanty and does not lend itself easily to certain decipherment. For the most part also it has less significance for religion than for anthropology, or in some instances for art. When the difficulties of interpretation have been surmounted, and a general agreement has been reached as to the value and meaning of the evidence thus to hand, it has not been found to contribute anything new or of permanent worth to the inferences drawn from the ideas and observances of existing tribes. There is no indication whatever that these prehistoric peoples were on a substantially lower level of civilisation than the savage and barbarous tribes of our own day. As far however as it can be satisfactorily interpreted and relied upon, the ancient evidence is in harmony with the modern and does not suggest any difference in the nature or line of development of ancient thought. The latter, however, is at a grave disadvantage in that in case of doubt it cannot be checked or revised in any way. If the ancient record, whatever form it has assumed, is blundered or misleading, there is no possibility of correcting it, and no means of escape from the errors into which it betrays us, except by ignoring altogether its witness. The living 'ribe on the other hand may be brought into court, their beliefs and usages tested at every point, the inferences tentatively drawn revised in the light of fuller and more accurate knowledge, and an ever clearer conception gained, as of a document that may be re-read at will. The evidence thus preserved in the ancient literature and monuments is not to be ignored or set aside, but it is at the best scanty and inferior to the modern, and needs discreet interpretation. So far as available it does in fact confirm the latter in all material respects.

There is thus a manifest advantage in the comparative enquiry into the beliefs of living tribes as compared with the records of the past. They are present and to hand for us to question at will. Even this more easy and promising investigation is beset with many difficulties. We cannot take it for granted that their beliefs represent any very close approximation to the beginnings of faith and religion. In many instances it is sufficiently clear that they do not; that behind them lies a considerable period of evolution and progress. Nor have we evidence sufficient to justify the assertion that the ancient historic or prehistoric peoples of whom we have any knowledge were in general at an earlier stage than they in the development of religious belief. In some cases it is possible, perhaps probable, that they were; in others the verdict must be one of "not proven." The only practicable course therefore is to examine and test the available evidence of every kind, and to endeavour to draw the conclusions that on the whole appear to have the best warrant. Of this evidence the modern is the more substantial and trustworthy.

Similarity of Primitive Beliefs

A further and not unimportant or irrelevant fact

is the close, almost surprising similarity which is found to exist between the primitive creed of all tribes, whether ancient or modern, and to whatever country they belong. Certain broad types or characteristics of belief are readily distinguishable; which may, or may not be reducible to one. The beliefs themselves however take on the same form, and manifest themselves under similar aspects. The gods for example, as they begin to emerge into distinctness and personality, will bear different names in the various countries in which primitive deities are worshipped—Mithra, Varuṇa, or Indra, Zeus, Jupiter, Wodan or Thor—but they are clothed essentially with the same high attributes, discharge substantially the same functions, and are regarded as holding like relations to mankind. Whatever the reason may be, the mind of man in its early endeavours to establish contact and communion with the unseen does not appear to have been characterised by variety of conception, but rather by a remarkable uniformity.

Three Principal Types

The leading types of early religious conception and faith are three. In the discussion or description of these it is inevitable that definite terms such as faith or belief should be employed with regard to them. There is a danger however lest the use of terms of this nature should suggest a more or less elaborate and fixed creed, and a firm border line that demarcates the belief in question from all other convictions or ideas. In reality nothing is more nebulous and floating than primitive conceptions; they are half-toned, and shade off into one another, so that it is often difficult if not impossible to determine where one class or type of belief ends and another begins. And were it practicable to secure from two individuals of a given savage or primitive tribe, with presumably similar conceptions of nature and the unseen, a complete and lucid description of the beliefs upon which their conduct in religious matters is based, it is most unlikely that the two descriptions would agree except in broadest outline; the details would be differently filled in, according to the reflective competence of the speaker and his facility of expression. The classification of creeds therefore is the work of the investigator, who sifts the raw material, often sufficiently crude and incoherent. The difficulties of the task are so considerable that each one of the types of belief to be enumerated has been regarded by influential and competent scholars as the source of the other two, and the ultimate origin or basis of religion itself. A triple classification is indeed far from exhausting the possibilities of detailed enumeration or division. It is summary and convenient rather than final, a working hypothesis, not a definitive and dogmatic and final scheme. It does not preclude or deny on the one hand the possible existence of other types, or on the other the hope or anticipation that the three may ultimately be reducible to two or even to one. The religious thought of man even in its beginnings is as various as the human mind itself, though the variety seems to be contained within narrow limits. It is practicable however, and will be useful to distinguish these three main types of primitive belief, and to recognise in them the chief modes in which the religious thought of man has endeavoured to find expression.

ANIMISM

Of the three probably the most important and widely influential is that which is known as "nature-worship," or "animism" if the latter term be accepted in its most general sense. The word has been employed however with varied and often quite indefinite connotation, and perhaps it would be preferable to avoid the use of it altogether, until some general agreement can be reached with regard to its precise import. The meaning intended to be conveyed by these or similar terms is that the impression made upon the mind of primitive man by the universe around him is that of an indefinite number of "animated" or self-acting powers, in a more or less intimate relation to himself, capable of affecting or controlling his life and well-being in practically every respect; towards which therefore—for they are hardly personified in the first instance—he adopts an attitude of reverence or "worship." Since, moreover, the only initiative or impulse to action of which he has any conscious experience proceeds from his own will, or inferentially from the wills of other men whom he assumes to be constituted like himself, to these active forces also he naturally ascribes a will and determination similar to his own. Their action however is on a far wider scale than his solitary and restricted efforts, more effective in its working, more destructive or beneficent in its consequences, more incalculable also and beyond prediction both in regard to the motive by which it is actuated and the results which will follow. Once again, therefore, primitive man finds ground for apprehension and "worship." The lightning may be prevailed upon not to strike, the destructive flood to pass by his dwelling, the tempest to abate its threatenings, the frost or burning heat to spare his crops. Of the unknown he is altogether fearful. Powers that too often appear to him to be malevolent and to take delight in injury, seem to hold him fast in a relentless grip. He is ever the plaything of their caprice. He is himself however amenable to gifts and moved by prayer; he will try the same process upon his "gods." Although it is only at a later stage of development that he learns to think of these forces as other than impersonal, that he defines them to himself as living beings, there is present from the beginning the attempt to place himself in right relationship with them, to deprecate their hostility and to secure their good-will. And in this we rightly see the early gropings of a religious instinct and endeavour.

Ultimately no doubt, this belief together with the resulting action is based upon analogy.* In every instance he himself acts, or apart from external constraint believes himself to act because he wills and determines thus to do. The forces of nature around him however work on a transcendently greater scale and with larger effects than lie within his personal and private competence. Naturally, therefore, he ascribes

* Cp. H. Höffding, *Philosophy of Religion*, p. 72: "If we want to convince ourselves that any other beings have a conscious life, analogy alone can supply us with a basis for this assumption."

to them a transcendently wider range of initiative control and will. In his attitude towards them he is definitely "religious."

This is "animism" in its rudest and most primitive expression. It naturally leads the way to a polytheistic type of faith, in which blind impersonal forces have become individual and distinct deities. This also is the most usual line of development. Among many savage peoples, however, traces of belief in a supreme Power, more distant and exalted, have been found, who interests himself but rarely if at all in the affairs of men. Evidence of the existence of such a belief has been accumulating within recent years by means of the researches of many students, and from countries as widely separated as Bengal and West Africa, and has been recorded also in Ceylon, Borneo, Madagascar, and ancient Rome. It does not appear, however, that worship is directly offered to these supreme Beings. The popular recognition of them amounts to little more than a dim consciousness of their existence. Though they are universally regarded as beneficent, requests for aid or good gifts are not generally addressed to them. The energies of the people in worship and offerings and prayer are reserved for the inferior deities, whose attitude is more uncertain, and from whose wrath much is immediately to be feared. It is on this account that the considerable place which deities of this character hold in early belief has been only gradually realised, and their position in the progress and development of religious faith is difficult to assess. Their dignity and might are unasserted, and in practice they show themselves indifferent to human affairs. The place therefore which they might be expected to occupy in the consciousness and thought of men is usurped by powers more likely to be prevailed upon to distribute benefit, or from whose vindictiveness or malice more is to be feared.

Shamanism and Fetichism

Forms of worship or religion more or less closely related to primitive animism are *Shamanism*, the religion of the witch-doctor or medicine man, and *Fetichism*, a widespread superstition whose home and most powerful seat is among the negro tribes of the West Coast of Africa. The distinctive feature of Shamanism is the recognition of a human intermediary, through whom the divine will is or may be communicated to those who seek counsel or relief. The name is derived from the ancient Sanskrit title (*śramaṇa*) for a Buddhist monk or ascetic. This is a prevailing type of religious belief in Northern and Central Asia, where Buddhism in the early and middle ages exercised so potent an influence; in its essentials, however, it represents a world-wide superstition and practice. By whatever name he is known, the Shaman, who lays claim to the possession of peculiar facilities of intercourse with the other world and the power to command at will the subservient intervention of the unseen powers, plays an important part in the social and religious life of most primitive peoples. His functions, however, are magical rather than religious in the stricter sense; and in any case are indicative of a state or stage of progress in religious thought considerably more advanced than the cruder animistic type.

Fetichism is a term introduced by the early Portuguese discoverers and traders on the West Coast of Africa to describe a form of religious or superstitious belief which they found prevailing among the tribes of that part of the continent. The fetich (Port. *feitiço*, from Lat. *factitius*) is a material object, which is conceived to possess inherent magical properties or powers, in virtue of which it is regarded with superstitious reverence or fear. The *tabu* of Polynesia represents an essentially similar conception, but associated rather with the living individual of peculiar separateness or sanctity, whose touch or word of command communicates holiness to whatsoever he pleases. The fetich, moreover, differs from an image or idol in that the latter is the visible representative or home of the god, while to the former is ascribed a mysterious faculty or force which is all its own, and is not due to the advent or residence of an external power.

Ancestor Worship

A second and very widely extended type or form of worship is that of the ancestor, whether of the individual or of the clan. Some authorities also have recognised in reverence for ancestors and the cult or practice thereon established the original source and origin of all religious creed and system. According to them religion in the broadest acceptation of the term has been developed out of a natural regard for the deceased parent or ancestor, which has found expression in rite and ceremony and prayer ; the ancestor is then deified, becomes a god, and the outlines of a religious system are ready to hand. For more reasons than one it is improbable that this view is correct. The fact that in a more or less well-defined shape ancestor-worship forms part of the faith and practice of nearly all peoples, ancient no less than modern, and is by no means confined to savage, uncivilised tribes, does not suffice to prove its primitive character. The cult of the ancestor clearly presupposes belief in the survival of the individual after death, and in the personal identity of the deceased with the previously living man. The catastrophe of death has not dissolved the continuity of personal existence. This conception, however, practically universal as it may be, can hardly be the root, the *fons et origo*, of the dimly conceived ideas that are involved in the rudimentary and impersonal beliefs of a primitive animism. The latter may conceivably be the source whence the former has originated and been developed; the contrary view is not tenable. What degree of relationship or interdependence exists between them is still to be investigated. The lines upon which they have respectively moved diverge, perhaps increasingly, with the progress of thought. Carried backward they certainly intersect, and may even coincide as religion's beginning and source is approached.

The underlying motive of the ancestral cult would appear to be two-fold: affection, expressing itself in an endeavour to promote the well-being of the deceased in the strange circumstances of the other world; or fear of his return to claim the place which was his before death but which another or others now fill, and of the revenge which he may be moved to take for the want of respect thus shown to him and to his memory. The mourning garments and the funeral feast, the provision by offerings made in or at the tomb for the sustenance of the dead man and to meet his varied needs in the new life upon which he has entered, are indications of the former mood and intention, and of a real desire to pay him due honour and to give proof of the love of those who survive him. The various devices by which it is sought to prevent the return of the ghost, to secure that he shall be well and truly buried beyond possibility of resurrection, or to mislead him if he should in spite of all precautions find his way back to haunt restlessly his former home and to disturb the inmates, prove how universal is the dread of the intangible and unseen. This fear of a possible mischievous activity of the deceased, to the hurt of his surviving relatives and friends, is a very prevalent motive among savage and primitive peoples; it is, however, in reality more closely akin to spirit-worship or animism in general than to a true ancestral cult. The real motive and basis of ancestor worship, as it is practised to the present day by the great nations of the East, in whose religious system and faith it is seen at its best, is undoubtedly the feeling of affection which sought to maintain continuity of personal and family or tribal intercourse with the dead, and to show to them to the fullest extent the reverence and honour which is theirs by right.

Totemism

In the third place is *totemism*, a no less widely-spread and influential form of belief among primitive races and tribes. Traces of totemism are to be found in the religious observances and cult of almost every nation, ancient and modern ; and at the present day a totemistic faith controls to a greater or less extent the practice and life of primitive tribes in North and South America, in Australasia and the islands of the Pacific, in India, China, and Japan, and among the negroes of the West Coast of Africa and the Bechuanas of the South. The term is employed to denote the peculiar theory or system of religious belief and usage which holds sacred a particular class of animate or inanimate objects, usually but not necessarily the former. In this case the totem will be some well-known animal, bird, plant, or insect, which the tribe or people reverence and by whose name they are usually known. Thus the bull or dog clan has for its totem the bull or dog respectively. Other clans, however, have adopted or inherited as their totem inanimate objects, as a rock, a stream, or one of the heavenly bodies ; or even an abstract term, as a day or month of the year. It would be preferable if the word could be restricted in its meaning to exclude these. It is, however, freely and somewhat loosely used to include types or examples of belief which are allied to totemism, although not really coincident with it in the more exact sense.

The word has been adopted from the language of the Ojibway Indians of North America, whose religious practices called attention in the first instance to totemism, and amongst whom the system appears to have reached its fullest development In almost every country, however, in which it is found it presents features that differ in some respects. In Australia, for example, the conditions and rules which regulate its application in the ordinary life of the aboriginal tribes are most complicated. There are three types or classes of totem: (1) the *clan* totem, which is common to every member of a clan or tribe; (2) the *sex* totem, held sacred by every male or female respectively of the tribe, but with no relation to the opposite sex; (3) the *individual* totem, the peculiar and private possession of a single individual, in which no other has a share. The second class has hitherto been recognised only in Australia, and doubtfully in England. From the totem animal the tribesman expects friendship and aid, and he will himself treat it in the same way with deference and regard; if wild or savage, it will not hurt him, and he on his part will refrain from injuring it. Under ordinary circumstances he will abstain also from eating its flesh, although he will sometimes kill it, in order to provide food for another. There is evidence that the ceremonial eating of the totem at sacrifices and feasts was formerly much more usual than at the present time. Moreover, on the occasion of festivals or special anniversaries the tribesman will sometimes dress himself in the skin of his totem, and thus arrayed will go through the prescribed ceremonies with dance and song. The totem name, therefore, is applicable to every member of a clan or tribe. The totem itself is one of a class, and is thus distinguished from the idol or fetich which is essentially and necessarily individual.

The difficulty of assigning a cause, or tracing the historical development of totemistic ideas is very great.

The underlying conception is probably that of a life shared in common by the human and animal creation. The spirit of man passes or may pass at death into the body of the animal; and at a future birth may resume human form. There is therefore between them a real sympathy and brotherhood which takes or should take the form of mutual helpfulness and support. Doctrinally, therefore, it is akin to the belief in the survival of the soul after death, and to theories of transmigration; and so far would seem to be ultimately traceable to animistic conceptions. It is impossible, however, to consider the question of the origin of totemism without taking acount of the family and social rules and ordinances associated with it. All totemistic tribes without exception as far as our knowledge goes are exogamous, and have more or less elaborate regulations which determine the intermarriage of the members of the different clans—a social code, which is as binding as any known among more civilised communities. Totemism, therefore, as a theory or mode of life may be said to have two entirely different aspects, a social and a religious. What the relation between these two is, or whether there is any relation at all which would justify the inference that the one is derived from the other, is wholly undetermined. It is difficult to believe that their universal co-ordination is fortuitous; it seems to be equally difficult to suggest an adequate reason for their conjunction. It would perhaps be preferable to connne the name of totemism to the system in its religious aspect and associations, and to find some other term to cover its social usages. Even so the difficulty of their constant union would remain, a difficulty that is not lightened by the appropriation of a separate title. The social practices whatever their origin can hardly be regarded as giving rise to primitive religious conceptions of so remarkable a nature. The implied order of thought appears inconceivable. On the other hand the religious or semi-religious ideas do not naturally furnish the basis for conclusions which define with stringency social habit and custom. Of the many theories or explanations that have been offered none is satisfactory. Some have been abandoned by their authors themselves. The intimate connection with animism and animistic thought appears certain Other relations are for the present obscure, and their elucidation and settlement remain as problems of the future.

Accepted Axioms of Primitive Belief

It would not be difficult further to classify and subdivide the various types of early religious thought and practice. The accepted textbooks render abundant assistance in this respect. For the purposes of comparison and of Comparative Religion it is however needless. It is along these main lines that with many wanderings and deviations the mind of man has moved in its search after God, in its attempt to elucidate and understand the meaning of the universe, to know its Creator and the method of its creation. Even the brief consideration here given will have sufficed to show that the conceptions which underlie these various theories and beliefs are neither unfamiliar nor unlike; that they are based in general upon certain axioms or prepossessions of thought, which to the mind of primitive man passed unquestioned, great as may have been the controversies raised over them in later times. To him they were axiomatic truths, which probably he would have found it difficult to formulate or express in words, but which determined his entire religious attitude and life. These beliefs expressed in their simplest form were essentially in the existence and reality of the unseen, of a power or powers external to himself, to which he could not afford to be indifferent, and which were not indifferent to him ; into right and profitable relations to these he endeavoured to place himself. Of the origin of this conviction he made no attempt to give an account ; to him it was intuitive, as much a matter of course as his own existence. The second axiom or presupposition was that of the survival of the soul after death. Not that he could define or set forth in exact terms his conception either of the soul or of death, or offer any solution of mysteries which pressed so hard upon later thinkers ; probably he never attempted the task of interpretation or felt its need. There was, however, something within him which in his belief would survive the dissolution of the body, and either in this or in some other world would continue an existence which he seems usually and naturally to have conceived as similar to the present. The kings and chieftains ruled, the warriors fought, the servants and handmaidens pursued their ordinary tasks of service, the craftsmen and traders wrought and bargained, the huntsmen enjoyed the pleasures of the chase. That was one widely prevalent conception of the future life, perhaps not the earliest or most primitive. In another the soul, naked and destitute, wandered in darkness, longing for the light and the joys of which it had been deprived. This belief in the survival of the soul was clearly not identical with a doctrine of immortality as usually understood, however naturally and logically it might, in some instances at least, anticipate it. The savage did not forecast an interminable future. It was enough for him that death did not end all. His thought hardly looked at first beyond a generation; those he had seen die were in some form or other still alive. The problem of a permanent life, which the later doctrine of metempsychosis assumed and attempted to resolve, did not present itself to him, and if presented would scarcely have been understood.

It is evident also that much lies behind these two fundamental beliefs, and is presupposed by them. A complete and final account of the origin of religion would have to take account of them and trace them to their beginnings. Hypothesis and conjecture have here been busy, but it cannot be said that a large measure of success or consensus of opinion has been attained. The solution of the problem is beyond the reach of our present knowledge, and perhaps beyond the grasp of the faculties of the human mind. Scientific enquiry at least must inevitably stop here, and neither has nor can have anything to do with theories and hypotheses to which experience lends no support. For the purposes of Comparative Religion these two beliefs are found to be fundamental, and to admit neither of proof nor of refutation. They are simply *data*, which the early religious thought of man assumes, and carries forward into all his system and creed. We must not read into them too much, least of all the finished thought of later days. To him they were entirely crude and indefinite, unformed and inarticulate. They are, however, the background of all his thinking, and the basis upon which is built up, painfully and by slow degrees, his religious faith.

PART II

Relations and Scope of Comparative Religion

Before passing on to consider the advantages that may be anticipated from a study of Comparative Religion it will be well to review briefly its relations to the chief religions of the world, and to endeavour to estimate the contribution which they make to religious teaching and thought. A full and detailed account of the great world faiths is impossible here; nor is it necessary for the present purpose. A summary of the leading doctrines which they profess, and of the ritual and observances which they have enforced, will serve to indicate their place in the comprehensive scheme of human belief, and to suggest the aspect or aspects of faith upon which they have laid stress. The science of Comparative Religion gathers its material from all sources, and no system of religious creed or practice, however amorphous it may be or limited in its range and the number of its adherents, is really negligible. It is natural however, to hope for most from a comparison of the larger faiths which have won assent from a not inconsiderable portion of the human race. The great religions of the world are generally stated to be four in number: Hinduism, Buddhism, Christianity, and Muhammadanism;

in the above chronological order of birth and development. A few pages have been added on Judaism, because of its importance in relation to Christianity. For these and other faiths which have borne witness to man's interest in the world beyond and his convictions with regard to the supernatural and the unseen—Zoroastrianism, Taoism, Confucianism, Shintoism, etc.—there are available competent and authoritative treatises which set forth their teaching and describe their organisation.* The science of Comparative Religion proceeds on the assumption that to none of these has there been denied the possession of a measure of truth, which they hold not always clearly or with unfaltering grasp. The truth in each of them is mingled with a proportion of error, but is capable of disentanglement by patient study, and the issue at stake is well worth the trouble involved in the process of testing and examination. This element of true belief and real substantial conviction has been as the salt of the system, preserving it from corruption, and fortifying it in some degree against degradation, mere uselessness, or positive mischief.

(1) COMPARATIVE RELIGION AND HINDUISM

From a comparative point of view it is often said that Hinduism has more to contribute to a real understanding of religion and of the meaning of the religious life than any other non-Christian faith, and may be expected to throw more light than any other upon the teaching of Christ Himself, Eastern as that was in all its presumptions and outlook. In not a few instances these antici-

* *See* the bibliography, *infra*, p. 135.

pations will be found to be justified. Of all faiths Christianity of course owes most to Judaism. Its Founder spoke and taught as a Jew, and upon the foundations of ancient Jewish belief and ordered code of law and ritual built up His world-wide gospel, "fulfilling" the law and the prophets (Matt. v. 17).

In many respects, however, the traditions and associations of his own faith would place the Hindu more in sympathy with the doctrine and standpoint of Christ than would be natural or easy to one brought up in the atmosphere either of present-day Judaism or of the ordinary life of the West. The Eastern character of the teaching of Christ has often been insisted upon; and this is so far true that an Eastern mind is better prepared than the Western by education and inherited conviction to assent to its postulates and to appreciate their far-reaching significance. Of the larger faiths of the world Hinduism is not only the most ancient and, profoundly shaken as it has often been, the most persistent and stable, but it is also the best representative of the Eastern spirit.

Religious Spirit of Hinduism

Here, however, reference should perhaps be made to a statement or objection that is sometimes encountered. It is asserted that Hinduism is not in reality a religion at all, but a somewhat amorphous collection of social customs and avoidances, sanctioned by ancient authority and enforced by general consent, which has maintained its ground for centuries by virtue of the prestige attaching to ancestral custom and rights; of which the system of caste, with all that it implies, is the mainstay and compelling force. That is no doubt true from a certain point of view. If by religion is to be understood merely a system of external rule and observance, or a rigid creed demanding acceptance and subscription from all, then it may reasonably be argued that Hinduism does not fulfil the definition. A Hindu, like a poet, is born, not made—*nascitur non fit* ; and within broad limits he may follow his own convictions and preferences with regard both to belief and manner of life, provided he does not violate caste rules ; and may throughout remain in the eyes of his compatriots an orthodox Hindu. If a strict creed is of the essence of a religious faith then the Hindu claim must be abandoned. In matters of belief a wide liberty is permitted. If, however, Hinduism is not a religion in this acceptation of the term, there is very much religion in Hinduism. Judged by its temper and quality rather than by the letter of the law the system is informed in all its better parts by a truly religious spirit, which often rises to a high level of sincerity and devotion. This of itself would justify its inclusion here. For the purposes of the science of Comparative Religion also its breadth of view and freedom from strict limitation is a real gain.

Early Indian Nature Worship

The earliest form of the religion of the peoples of India, as it is made known to us in their ancient literature, is a rich and highly diversified nature worship ; a religious system and devotion which on the one hand is sufficiently near to the origin for the gods and goddesses to have preserved their primitive character, as representing the forces and phenomena of nature; and on the other has made considerable progress in the elaboration of an ethical ideal which enforces the claims of righteousness and justice, and the dependence of man upon his god. The deities worshipped are personifications of the powers of nature in the midst of which the Aryan peoples found themselves, and to which they attributed purpose and will, a definite character and mind. This personification, however, retained so much of transparency that it never obscured or concealed the natural basis upon which it rested. Almost all the deities moreover are beneficent and kindly—a tribute to the gentle and humane character of the Indians themselves, who naturally pictured their gods in their own image. Vindictiveness and malevolence are the qualities of the demons who in great numbers haunt both earth and air to do what harm they may; with whom the gods are at perpetual strife. Perhaps the most prominent feature of the worship is the reverence paid to the sun in many phases and forms. Solar worship also has maintained its position and importance in Indian households to the present day. In primitive times it is not to be wondered at that the scorching power of the sun's rays as they dried up and seared the land exacted from man a superstitious respect and dread. Magic spells to avert the evil eye, talismans to frustrate the devices and malice of the demons, charms to heal diseases, were at least as common as hymns in praise of the goodness of the gods, or petitions for their favour and gifts. In other directions also these early Indian writers proved themselves advanced in religious apprehension and thought. They seem to have formulated already some dim and naïve theory of inspiration. The authors of the hymns "saw" the verses and words which they communicated to men. The framers of the theory, if theory it may be called, intended the phrase of course to signify mental or spiritual vision. A later generation interpreted it literally of the bodily eye, and supposed that through literal physical sight the inspired word reached their minds.

Further it must be remembered that the literature in which these doctrines and thoughts are enshrined cannot be considered as representing a definitely limited period or the systematised faith of a particular locality. Apart from the uncertainty as to the date of the writers themselves, there can be little doubt that its composition extended over several centuries. It represents in general the beliefs and practices of the Panjāb and the North-west of India. But doctrines which lie side by side in the literature as it has been transmitted to us, and which appear to us to form a coherent whole, may in reality be separated by considerable intervals of time or place. There is, however, little indication of movement or growth and progress of thought in the oldest stratum of the literature. For all practical purposes it may be regarded as giving expression to a definite and early stage of religious development and belief.

Polytheism and Henotheism

Two or three further characteristics of this early scheme of thought and faith are worthy of notice. They are for the most part features of all nature worship, but accentuated in the Indian system. There is a two-fold tendency observable in regard to the number and functions of the gods themselves; in the first place, a movement towards multiplicity, polytheism, which eventually led to the creation of the immense pantheon of India's gods. Under any nature system it is easy to establish new divinities. Over against this, however, and in a certain measure counteracting it, was set the habit or principle, which is known as *henotheism* or *kathenotheism*, the recognition of one deity at a time as supreme, with no claim or right however to perpetuity of tenure. He is readily displaced by another, as the caprice or will of the worshipper may dictate. Logically this principle would seem to point the way to monotheism, a temporary authority and sway being converted to permanent dominion, and the subordinate deities being gradually divested of all separate functions and ultimately of existence itself. In India at least this step was never taken. The polytheistic tendency proved to be possessed of superior vitality and strength. Fresh divinities continually appeared; and the process has by no means ceased at the present day.

Ethics

It is noteworthy also that in most of this early literature stress is laid upon moral claims and personal character. The gods are on the side of justice and right, and purity and sincerity of heart are necessary conditions of all acceptable worship. The ritual, the mere act of sacrifice, was in many instances at least regarded as inefficacious unless it was accompanied by prayer, the uplifting of the heart in sincere desire and supplication. This is all the more worthy of notice, because the better side of the ritual of offering was so soon obscured and lost. The offering itself became a mere bargain, a price paid to secure a coveted benefit; and the prayer a spell, or magical utterance, without which the presentation of the offering and the performance of the rite would fail of their effect. Irrespective of its meaning, or of the character or intention of the offerer, the word itself came to be conceived as possessed of compelling power. In all this it is easily seen how far early Hindu religion had in reality moved from the convictions and simplicity of primitive faith.

Ritual

Within a few centuries this intimate worship of the gods, to all appearance perfectly loyal and sincere, was exchanged, under the influence of a dominant priesthood, for a system of ritual and sacrifice, in which the performance of the rite under the guidance of the officiating priest took the place of the frank and open approach to the gods. No ethical demand was now made upon the worshipper. The emphasis was laid upon the act itself, the strict and regular manner in which it was performed, not upon the spirit in which it was undertaken. The attitude and character of the worshipper was of no moment, only the legal propriety and perfectness of the ritual. And a close corporation of priests undertook the formulating of the rules and the superintendence of the acts by which the ritual was carried out; constituting themselves in fact intermediaries between man and his god. A more fatal arrest of development or one more deadening to the religious spirit it is difficult to imagine. The ordinary man was denied direct access to the deity. He could only approach through and with the aid of the priest, and, himself without responsibility or power, the acceptance of his offering and the efficacy of his prayer were entirely dependent upon the good will and inerrancy of his sponsor at the altar or in the home. It was a religion of externals, of form and ceremony, from which the spirit had gradually flickered out and finally disappeared.

Eschatology

During this period of change and development, the length of which must certainly be measured by centuries, there had been considerable advance in doctrine, one element of which alone need be referred to here, representing as it does a transition stage to a most important and characteristic article of Indian faith. The earlier literature pays slight regard to the conditions of existence after death. In a general way it is affirmed that the good enjoy felicity with the gods, the wicked pass into a state of darkness and misery in the world below. Neither of the one nor the other, however, is the status which he enjoys, or the character and quality of the future life precisely set forth; nor is any attempt made to determine its limit. Later there emerges a well-defined doctrine of future rewards and punishments, the righteous are recompensed after death for and on account of their good deeds, the wicked suffer the penalty of their crimes. Together with this doctrine of retribution there is formulated for the first time a theory of re-birth, a return of the soul to this world, again to pass through the cycle of birth, maturity, old age and death. The return, however, is neither universal nor compulsory, two features in which it is distinguished from the more consistent and finished theory of later times. Of the derivation and origin of this remarkable doctrine no certain account can be given; and its relation to the parallel but independent teaching of an after-life of reward or punishment is obscure. Important contributions, moreover, of doctrine and belief have yet to be made to it before it assumes its final shape in the theory of transmigration, familiar to all students of Indian thought.

THEISM AND PHILOSOPHY

Nature worship and the reverence for the deities of the country-side have never lost their hold upon the village population in general. In the higher circles of speculation and thought, however, theistic and metaphysical doctrines were expounded, which profoundly modified the substance of Indian belief. It is probable that these were to a considerable extent in conscious opposition to the accepted doctrine of the ritual and to the ascendancy of the priests. Moreover in India philosophy has rarely if ever been divorced from religion; it has been the handmaid or ally of the latter, not its rival or foe; and no comparative view of India's religious beliefs can ignore or omit to take account of her philosophical creed. The Indian mind is essentially and profoundly metaphysical in its tendency. Inquiries into the nature of being and the universe present to it great attractions, and have formed the basis of very varying theories of the constitution, history and destiny of the world and of men. A brief reference to the philosophical scheme or theory which has taken the leading place in Indian thought is all that is here possible.

Idealism

In general the speculative thought of India has moved in the two directions of idealism and materialism. The latter in some of its more important developments would more fitly be described as agnosticism. Idealistic principles, however, have on the whole most commended themselves to the Hindu mind, and they are invariably found in alliance with definite religious beliefs. The most widely accepted theory is known as the *Vedānta*, an extreme monistic doctrine, which identified all with the one. Its watch-word was non-duality, there is one only existence or being in the universe, without another or a second. It follows that the Vedānta system denies all separate individuality. All souls are one with the great supreme soul, who or which alone exists. No attempt was made to describe or to account for this sole existent one, for whose title or name an abstract word in the neuter gender was employed; nor was it conceived or defined in any terms of personality. It simply "was" in the beginning, and there neither is nor ever has been nor can be another. As a corollary, which perhaps was not distinctly formulated until later times, the universe of form and matter is unreal, it has no true existence and only seems to be. Insight into this truth and acceptance of this doctrine was declared to be the only condition of salvation. Bondage was a bondage to ignorance (*avidyā*), and deliverance was achieved not by doing or by becoming something other than from the beginning, but by the removal of the veil, by realising the soul's identity with the unchanging eternal one.

It was understood, however, that this doctrine, highly refined and metaphysical as it was, was beyond the reach of ordinary men, who could not be expected to appreciate its significance or appropriate its truths. For them a method or department of works (*karmakāṇḍa*) was provided, that in the due observance of the rites and the offering of sacrifice they might find salvation. This was a secondary and inferior way of deliverance. The superior way was that of knowledge (*jñānakāṇḍa*), which was realisable, however, only by the elect few. Sometimes the relation between the two was defined in terms of symbolism. The external ritual was symbolic of higher truths, set forth in this form for the benefit of unlearned and ignorant men. Those who could receive the higher knowledge had no need of the ritual.

The Vedānta and the New Testament

A comparison has sometimes been instituted between this two-fold teaching of the ancient Indian literature on the one hand, and the doctrines enforced in the Old and New Testament Scriptures on the other. There is a similar insistence on the one side on something to be done, rites to be observed, sacrifices offered; and righteousness consists more or less in the exact and correct fulfilment of the conditions of the ritual: on the other on a doctrine or truth to be accepted and believed. There is to be noted, however, in the first instance a difference in the spirit in which the ritual is approached. There is little ethical content or demand in the Indian doctrine. The act itself is all important, and its efficacy is practically independent of the spirit in which it is undertaken. In the Jewish teaching a strong moral claim is made, moral conditions are enforced, and apart from moral rectitude of heart and life it is made clear that mere outward observance is of no avail. A more deep-seated contrast exists between the principles of the *jñānakāṇḍa* and those of the New Testament writers. In the former salvation depends upon knowledge; it is not a change of character or disposition, of heart or aim that is demanded, but the recognition of a fact. "Know this," *i.e.* the identity of the human soul with the divine, and in and with that knowledge deliverance is secure. In the New Testament the emphasis is laid upon the character and will. Knowledge indeed is indispensable, the knowledge of God and of His purpose and plan. But the first and essential condition is the reversal of the will to do evil, and the accession of a will to do and to be good. It might not unfairly be said that the difference between the two systems of thought is comprehended in these two words, knowledge and will. The difference of principle is far-reaching and profound.

Progressive Doctrine of Transmigration

There is advance also in regard to the doctrine of transmigration of souls, to which reference has already been made. That doctrine received in India its most comprehensive form and statement. Of the history of its development, however, or of the source of the doctrine itself and the successive contributions or accretions which gave it final shape and consistence, little is known. In the earliest literature and popular belief, as has been indicated above, no true doctrine of transmigration appears. Later the belief in a reincarnation after death is found concurrently with the normal teaching of felicity or woe in another world. Such reincarnation, however, is neither compulsory nor universal, and the conditions under which it takes place are not clearly defined.

In the final form of the doctrine re-birth in this world is part of the natural order of the universe, and is necessary and inevitable for all living beings. Justice moreover is satisfied by the law that the conditions of the renewed earthly life are automatically and precisely determined by the previous deeds and character of the individual. The good man is rewarded by birth into a higher scale of being, the grade of which is determined by the number and quality of his good deeds. The evildoer suffers for the evil that he has wrought, and the penalty exacted in the new existence is accurately proportioned to the degree of his guilt. The theory would seem thus to be complete, and incapable of any material extension; nor, in fact, has it undergone any further change or modification in Indian thought. It is universally accepted as the principle or basis of human life, and the sufficient explanation of all anomalies in the distribution of joy or suffering, of good and evil fortune,

Every man receives the portion which he merits; and his lot in life is precisely determined by his deserts. The doctrine, moreover, does not limit the possibilities or sphere of re-birth to the human creation. It includes animals and all living beings, and even inanimate things as trees and stones. The changes are rung on all created things, from the lowest to the highest, whether animate or wholly material.

Hindu Thought Pantheistic and Theistic

It might fairly be contended that these later movements of religious and philosophical thought have found their sphere among the more leisured classes but are not likely to have touched the lower, whose practical needs are summed up in the endeavour to satisfy the urgent claims of the body. That is not entirely so in India. The essential religiousness of the Hindu and his thoughtful mysticism have disposed him to probe deeply into the problems of God and the universe and of man's relation to both, where other people through indolence or mental inefficiency have stayed their steps on the threshold. The Indian peasant is a philosopher, as well as a man of religious faith. And if not always able to give a reason for the faith that is in him, he has often sincerely and steadily endeavoured to think out these things, and the creed in which he has been nurtured has taken strong hold of his imagination and his heart. It is this religiousness which explains the force and persistence of the theistic conception and worship from the earliest times. The general assertion that Indian philosophic thought is predominantly pantheistic is justified as the brief preceding consideration will have shown. By the side, however, of the pantheistic assumption there has always existed a strain of theism or even monotheism of very considerable if not equal antiquity. Its origin is uncertain both as regards date and place; but it was independent both of the rigidly orthodox creed and of the patronage of the priests. Later it entered into agreement with them, with mutual borrowings and adaptations, and by its widespread popularity and influence has proved itself to be responsive to the Indian mind and heart. Probably it was never more widely and fruitfully influential than at the present day. By some writers a Christian source and origin have been claimed for a system and creed that in some of its features greatly resembles Christianity. It is probable that in its later stages it came into contact with Christian teaching, and its creed locally at least was influenced by Christian thought. In its initiation and early stages, however, it was of purely Indian conception and derivation. Before the Christian era began it had passed through some centuries probably of gradual progress and expansion. Whatever debt may have been incurred in later times to Christian associations the initial conception and amplifications were worked out in Indian minds and were native to the Indian soil.

Theism

This theistic movement found expression in the so-called popular religions of the country, which have divided between them the allegiance of the great majority of the peoples of India. In origin, though not in name or form, they are little if at all more recent than the most ancient literature. Later they allied themselves with the philosophical schools, so that it is not easy to determine with regard to either of them where the religion ends and the philosophy begins. The mythology of their deities and the ideals of their faith were enshrined in the great epic poems and kindred literature, the major portion of which is of comparatively recent origin but which comprise elements certainly antedating the Christian era. The eloquence and music of the poetry, the attractiveness and beauty of many of the legends and characters have captivated the Indian heart; and told and retold in the villages, they have become inwoven into the memory and heart of the people. In particular, the *Bhagavadgītā* or *Gītā*, the "Song" or "Song of the Blessed" or "Worshipful One," has often been designated the New Testament of the Hindus, and gives expression to sentiments and aspirations, to which universal judgement would assign a high place of permanent worth. "When I am lonely," a wandering Indian ascetic declared, "I read in my copy of the Bhagavadgītā and get consolation, and I like that better than any other book, because it makes my heart glad." Once again Christian influence has been suspected. It cannot be proved, however, that Christian teaching has modified in any way the natural development of the doctrine of the Gītā. The contrary has been maintained, that the thought and even the phraseology of the Gītā have passed into the New Testament. In its extreme form neither claim is justified. But the history of the intercourse between the two faiths in India in the early and middle centuries is little known. In its later stages the same therefore may be said of the Gītā as of Indian theism in general that the partial assimilation of Christian ideas and doctrines is not improbable. In origin, however, the faiths of India and of Palestine were independent.

Asceticism

A very marked and characteristic feature, moreover, of Indian religion from the earliest times has been the ascetic tendency. The voluntary hardships and self-inflicted tortures of the ascetics of India have surpassed anything that the West has known. The principle of asceticism, perhaps more definitely in India than elsewhere, assumes and involves theistic belief. The ascetic desires, and by the way of subjection of the body endeavours to achieve union with a personal god. The importance of the concentration of the mind upon God, desiring union with Him, is more emphasized in the Indian textbooks and in practice than any self-mortification; the latter is only useful as it promotes the former. Theoretically, also, every Brāhman or high caste Hindu should, towards the close of life, dissociate himself from worldly possessions and engagements, and become a wandering, homeless ascetic, seeking in solitary meditation and prayer that fellowship and union with the Divine to the attainment of which worldly cares have always been found to be an obstruction and a hindrance. There are further remarkable and in some instances unique features of Indian asceticism which make it worthy of study, notably its dreamy pantheistic mysticism, and the belief that by intense concentration of thought and mastery of the bodily passions magical properties and powers of the most extensive order may be assured. This may be regarded as illustrating the close relationship and frequent alliance between magic and religion. The wide prevalence however of ascetic practices in India, and the popularity of the ascetic life give proof again of the strong hold which theistic belief has upon the heart and conscience of the people.

Other prominent features of Hindu religious life are the multiplicity of female deities with the prevalence of mother-worship; and the reverence for the *Guru* or religious teacher. The latter exercises an almost unbounded influence, often over a considerable area of country; under normal conditions no serious step would be taken without his concurrence and advice.

Reform Movements

Moreover the history of Hinduism has been marked by the recurrence of reform movements, which have arisen from within in protest against the decadence or errors of orthodox teaching, but in many, perhaps most instances have been indebted for incentive and stimulus to the teaching and example of a more fresh and virile faith from without. Such was Buddhism before the beginning of our era, the earliest and perhaps the greatest of them all, and the movement initiated in the Panjāb by Kabīr in the fifteenth century. The latter received much of his doctrine and inspiration from Muhammadanism, and from out of the best elements of belief and practice in the two faiths sought to build up an eclectic system which should combine the merits and advantages of both. Christianity is said to have greatly influenced the native Indian reformers of the eleventh and following centuries; in some instances there can be little doubt that the assertion or claim is justified. In the nineteenth century, again, the founders of the Brāhma Samāj and other theistic Reformed Churches confessedly owed much to the teaching of the New Testament, and never attempted to conceal their reverence for the character of Christ. For the most part Hinduism has triumphed over these essays at reformation, and has succeeded in maintaining in their despite its own position and social order. Their history has presented in this respect a considerable though not complete uniformity. A period of freshness and vigour, with a more or less extensive and successful campaign of proselytism, has been followed by a slackening of effort and a gradual relapse into customs, and revival of usages and beliefs, against which their earlier leaders and teachers had entered an emphatic protest. It was all perhaps natural enough. But it proved the strength of the Hindu position, even if it was predominant by the force of inertia and established prestige.

(2) COMPARATIVE RELIGION AND BUDDHISM

The institution of a comparison between Buddhism and other faiths, together with a comparative estimate of their merits and defects, is rendered more difficult by the extreme complexity of the system or systems that pass under that name. That the Buddhist contribution to the sum total of human knowledge and thought has been not inconsiderable will hardly be denied. Its ethical code is of a high order; its religious worth has greatly impressed many who have studied it at first hand, and in its own homes. On the other hand, as to Hinduism so to the Buddhist faith has been denied the right or claim to the name of a religion in the true sense—on the ground that it presents for acceptance a philosophical and moral system, dissociated from any real religious element. The Buddhist claim however is not difficult to substantiate. The objection rests upon a mistaken estimate of the scope and character of Buddhist beliefs. These are in reality neither of the simplicity nor of the somewhat cold and strict severity that has often been attributed to them. The articles of the Buddhist faith are as diverse and almost as widely comprehensive as those of Hinduism, and offer as many sharp contrasts as those of the various Christian Churches. If these last may be brought under one name and title by virtue of their faith in Christ, a similar attachment to and belief in the Buddha may be held to knit together the different forms of Buddhism. The link however is perhaps slighter, and for practical purposes less effective in the case of the latter than of Christianity.

Schools of Thought

There are two leading schools of Buddhist thought and belief, and a comparative estimate of these is as essential for the student of Comparative Religion as an analysis of the resemblances or divergences between

Buddhism and Christianity. For the present it is better to defer the comparison until the principal doctrines of the sects that will enter into consideration have been reviewed. The two schools are known as the Hīnayāna and the Mahāyāna. They are far apart in principles and theory of life, and from many points of view might not unreasonably be regarded as distinct and separate faiths. It is between the latter of these, the Mahāyāna, and Christianity that resemblances have been asserted to exist sufficiently close to render a theory of the independence in their entirety of the two religions extremely improbable. If historically and in the course of their growth and development borrowing has taken place, it will be necessary to attempt to determine on which side the debt has been incurred. Christianity and Buddhism do in fact stand nearer together and are in more real and intimate sympathy than Buddhism and any other faith. In moral and ethical precept especially they are nearly akin, and the likeness in this respect can hardly escape the notice even of the most superficial observer. To what extent direct borrowing on either side may be assumed to be at the basis of the admitted agreement is another and more difficult question.

Early Buddhism Protestant

Like many other movements of reform, Buddhism had its origin in a protest against a religion of externals, of ritual form and calculated service, whereby at so much cost deliverance might be secured from the pains and penalties of existence in the present world—a protest against what Hinduism had learnt to know as *karma-kāṇḍa*, the way of works, which taught that in the performance of a strict ritual man might find salvation. Of this method the Buddha himself is said to have made trial, practising for a lengthened period the severest asceticism in the hope that freedom might be gained through subjection of the body. When this failed he sought and found deliverance and enlightenment by the way of meditation and concentration of thought, pondering over the mysteries of being and the means by which evil and suffering might be overcome and rest and peace attained. According to the tradition insight came to him in a moment, as he sat in thought under the sacred Bo-tree. In Christian phraseology he was "converted," and thenceforth devoted his life to preaching and teaching the doctrine and truth of which he believed himself thus to have become possessed.

Foundation and Early Progress

The Buddhist books give details of his subsequent itinerant life, of the discourses which he delivered, and of the creed or doctrines which he commended to his disciples. How far the Buddhist theory and teaching in their final form, as presented in the literature, were due to Gautama himself, or how far a nucleus of doctrine was elaborated and completed by his successors, it is impossible to determine. His personal efforts and propaganda are represented as might be anticipated as eminently successful, and very large numbers of disciples are said to have gathered around him. There is no real evidence however of the position or influence of the faith in India during his life time, nor in the immediately succeeding period, until it was adopted nearly three centuries later by the Emperor Aśoka (reigned 273 to 231 B.C.), who, with much zeal and success, propagated it throughout his dominions, and sent missionaries into many of the surrounding countries. To Aśoka has been given sometimes the title of the Constantine of Buddhism; and a similar controversy has been waged in his case over the question whether his influence and patronage have proved eventually to be for the benefit and furtherance of the true interests of the religion which he professed. Probably his life and work were more significant and effective for Buddhism than those of his rival on behalf of the Christian faith. At his death Buddhism was the established and prevailing religion over the greater part of India, and had found more or less a welcome and a home in many neighbouring lands. How far the adherence to the royal faith was intelligent and sincere, we have no means of judging. Certainly, however, the earnest zeal and efforts of the Emperor gave to the faith an impulse and a popularity from which for many centuries there was no decline. Aśoka well merits the title of the second founder of Buddhism. To his example as well as to his precept its success and rapid growth were due. His edicts bear every mark of sincerity and of an earnest solicitude for the moral as well as the material good of his people.

It has usually been assumed that before his conversion to Buddhism Aśoka was an orthodox Hindu. No direct evidence as to his earlier faith is available. On slender grounds it has been conjectured that he was a Jaina, a member of the religious system and creed contemporary in its origin with Buddhism and so remarkably akin. More recently the suggestion has been made of Persian or Zoroastrian influence on the dynasty to which the Emperor belonged. The suggestion is based upon archæological evidence, and Aśoka himself is further supposed to have been originally a Zoroastrian. The evidence thus far adduced falls short of demonstration. The possibility however of such influence must be admitted, and a feasible explanation would then be afforded of features in the Buddhist teaching, which are not altogether easily interpreted from native Indian sources. The point is not unimportant, as tending to elucidate the sources and relations of Buddhist doctrine. Attention has also been redirected to the name of the clan to which Gautama Buddha himself belonged, who, according to the tradition, were overwhelmed and annihilated not long after the death of the great Teacher. If the tribal name of Śākya is to be connected historically with Śaka and the invasion of India from the north, then the theory of its Scythian or Iranian origin would to that extent be justified. There is reason to hope that further and satisfying evidence may be brought forward in the course of investigation and study.

The circumstances of the Buddha's attainment of wisdom involved a long and terrifying conflict with the powers of evil. Māra the tempter used every device and exerted all his strength to turn him from his purpose. The details of his assaults are narrated in the Buddhist books, and these are accompanied by exaggerated and monstrous exertions of magical power. During the night following the discomfiture of Māra and his hosts, the truth is revealed to Gautama seated in meditation under the Bo-tree. According to one form of the tradition he remained thereafter fasting for seven weeks "enjoying the bliss of emancipation." Each of the long series of Buddhas who preceded Gautama is said to have passed through similar experiences, and to have attained finally to a knowledge of the truth under a sacred tree. Each in turn devoted himself to the proclamation of the truth which he had thus learned; and in each case the religious system which he founded passed through phases of increase and prosperity followed by decadence and decay, and ultimately disappeared from the earth. Thus Buddhism itself does not contemplate permanence. Tradition has preserved the prophecy of the Founder concerning its gradual decay and end. In due time there will appear upon the earth a future Buddha, who will restore the reign of righteousness and truth.

Buddhist Scriptures

As for early Hindu beliefs so for Buddhist history and doctrine dependence is necessarily placed upon the native literature. The sacred books of the Southern Buddhists are known as the *Tripiṭaka*, or "triple basket," consisting of three parts or sections which deal respectively with "discipline" or the rules and regulations for the monastic life; "doctrine" or discourse, a series of expository and doctrinal statements in the form of sermons addressed by the Buddha to his disciples; and a third or supplementary section, the subject-matter of which is not essentially different from the second, including treatises on Buddhist philosophy and metaphysics; it is in general later in date and composition than the other two. The difficulty of drawing valid conclusions from these books with reference to the origin and development of doctrine is enhanced by the uncertainty as to their date. They are all alike in intention and form, and in the belief of the Buddhists themselves, the exact deliverances of Gautama himself. While they contain, however, much that is ancient in substance and teaching, it seems undeniable that they have undergone reconstruction and elaboration at various times to so considerable an extent that it is not easy to disentangle the new from the old. Some of the oldest material is found in the so-called Birth-Stories (*Jātaka*), which are professedly records of the sayings and doings of the Buddha in his former lives. Much of the folklore and many of the stories embodied in them are of great antiquity; some of the latter have found their way over a large part of Asia and Europe, and are familiar in modern collections of tales. The Christian legend of Barlaam and Josaphat, for example, is directly traceable to an Indian original in the Jātaka; and the latter contains an early Christian Apology borrowed from the Greek, an apologue or parable closely resembling the parable of the Sower in the Gospels, and the original of Shakespeare's story of the caskets in the "Merchant of Venice."

On the ethical side, the most instructive and typical of Buddhist writings is the *Dhammapada*, a treatise contained in the second "basket," consisting of a collection in twenty-six chapters of moral sayings or precepts, many of which recur in other parts of the Buddhist Canon. The work has been translated into many languages, and merits the attention of every student of religious or ethical thought. It is worth while to give a few extracts in illustration, but the whole book deserves study. The shrewd insight and wisdom of some of its sayings are very remarkable.

"If one man conquer in battle a thousand times a thousand men, and if another conquer himself, the latter is the greatest of conquerors."

"One's own self conquered is better than all other people; not even a god, a Gandharva, not Māra himself with Brahman could change into defeat the victory of a man who has vanquished himself, and always lives under restraint."

"Hatred does not cease by hatred at any time; hatred ceases by love, this is an old rule."

"As a grass-blade, badly grasped, cuts the arm, so badly-practised asceticism leads to hell."

"A man is not learned because he talks much; he who is patient, free from hatred and fear, he is called learned."

An entire chapter is given up to a description of the perfect man, the true Brāhmaṇa. It suggests a high conception of the ethical standard of probity and sincerity of character demanded of the early Buddhists.

"A man does not become a Brāhmaṇa by his plaited hair (*i.e.*, as an ascetic), by his family or by birth; in whom there is truth and righteousness, he is blessed, he is a Brāhmaṇa."

"What is the use of plaited hair, O fool! what of the raiment of goat-skins? Within thee there is ravening, but the outside thou makest clean."

"Him I own indeed a Brāhmaṇa who calls nothing his own, whether it be before, behind or between, who is poor, and free from the love of the world."

NORTHERN CANON

Other books were accepted by the Northern Buddhists as sacred and authoritative. Their Canon was indeed less strictly defined, and the works which they acknowledge hold no definite relation to one another, and can hardly be said to form a closed Canon in the technical sense. These works are all of North Indian origin, and were carried thence by Buddhist missionaries into the new homes of the faith, and translated from Sanskrit into the languages of the various countries into which Buddhism made its way. The books of the Southern Canon are however known and recognised everywhere, but are apparently little read. The Northern treatises for the most part expatiate on the delights of the Paradise of the West, describe the virtues and unbounded compassion of Amitābha, its great Lord, or following more closely on the lines of Indian philosophy present a reasoned defence of some point of doctrine or metaphysic. There is no settled Mahāyānist Canon, comparable for instance to the Hindu Vedas or the Christian Bible. Each country has its own collection in its own language, some works being common to all, and the remainder treating substantially of the same subjects, modified or coloured by the idiosyncrasies and capabilities of the people to whom they belong.

Missions

A further characteristic of early Buddhism was its intense and fervent missionary spirit. The itinerant work of Gautama Buddha himself and of the earlier disciples was propagandist and missionary in the widest and most liberal sense. And the Emperor Aśoka when he commissioned his envoys and preachers of the doctrine to carry the message to foreign rulers and lands was fulfilling on a larger scale the purpose of the founder. The most distant countries were successively evangelised —Tibet, China, Korea, Japan, in the north—Ceylon, Burma, and the islands of the Pacific in the south and east. In the west also the Panjāb and the borders of Afghanistan became strongholds of the Buddhist faith. There are indications, which perhaps hardly amount to proof, that Buddhist monks penetrated even to Egypt, and preached in the streets of Alexandria. And recent explorations and discoveries in Central Asia have proved how deep and strong was the hold of Buddhism over all that vast area. A reflex missionary interest is found in the journeyings and experiences of the Chinese pilgrims, who in the early centuries of the Christian era visited the sacred places of their religion in the north of India for the purpose of study and to secure copies of Buddhist books. The records of their travels, of the perils they faced and the sufferings they endured, have hardly been surpassed in variety and romance by any missionary literature of a later age. Of the three great missionary religions of the world, Buddhism is little if at all inferior to any in the extent and permanence of its conquests; and in its earlier days was fully the equal of its rivals in efficiency and zeal. A distinction, which is all to the honour of the Indian religion, is that in its propaganda Buddhism never employed the methods of persecution. So far as we know, Buddhist monks and preachers sought to persuade but never to compel. Violence and persecution were contrary to the precepts of their faith; and in this instance at least, precept was uniformly translated into practice.

Doctrinal Teaching

How far what may be called the essential and characteristic doctrines of Buddhism are really primitive and may be ascribed to the teaching and exposition of Gautama himself it is difficult to determine. It is hardly probable that a statement of doctrine, which on his lips, if the traditional accounts may be accepted, proved immediately convincing and attractive on a large scale, was other than simple, not burdened or complicated by metaphysical subtleties. He presented a truth which was easily apprehensible and offered relief to all. Upon the basis of his teaching later students and scholars built up elaborate systems of practical conduct and philosophic dogma. To distinguish with certainty between the earlier and later strata of theory and creed is not possible. In the Buddhist books, themselves more often than not of uncertain date, from which all our information is derived, the whole is attributed to the Buddha himself. He founded his teaching upon the ancient Indian doctrine of the essential unhappiness and impermanence of all existence, and declared that he had found the way of escape, which was open to all who would follow in his steps. This doctrine he enunciated in the so-called "Four Noble Truths" (*āryasatyāni*): all existence involves suffering; suffering is caused by desire, especially the desire for continuance of existence; the suppression of desire, therefore, will lead to the extinction of suffering; this is to be accomplished by the way of the Noble Eight-Fold Path—which he then proceeds to expound and enforce. This last is sometimes known as the Middle Path, because it avoids the two extremes of bodily indulgence and self-mortification or asceticism. The *āryasatyāni* are not altogether original. They are found stated in similar form, for example, in ancient Indian philosophy. The original element or elements appear to have been the stress laid upon immediate deliverance through and in the apprehension of these truths, and the unrestricted proclamation of them to all, high and low, rich and poor, without limitation of caste or sex, to be received and appropriated by all at will on equal terms.

A further formula of doctrine which, essentially at least, may in all probability be ascribed to Gautama himself is the brief Buddhist "Confession of Faith," the mere recitation of which is said to have aroused immediate conviction in the minds of some who became the foremost leaders of the early Buddhist community: "laws or conditions of existence that arise from a cause, the cause of these the Buddha declared, and also the cessation of them. Such truths the great Teacher uttered." It is on the basis of declarations of this nature that the materialistic character of Buddhism has been so frequently affirmed, and also the atheistic views of its founder. The question or questions present great difficulty, and cannot be argued out here. Whatever the precise bearing of primitive doctrine, however, modern Buddhism as professed and followed for the most part and by the great majority of its adherents is neither atheistic nor materialistic. Gautama himself is assumed to have held views that were agnostic. He certainly denied the existence of a "soul"; and to all demands for information with regard to the future after death he consistently refused to yield. It is more than doubtful whether this refusal was based upon agnostic grounds. It is not inconsistent with clear convictions of his own on these subjects, and it is altogether probable that he believed himself to possess adequate knowledge. The disciples had enough to do to order their conduct rightly in this world, and to ensure their own salvation, without busying themselves with curious speculation as to the next, and he therefore withheld information, which would have been of no present or practical utility. With the denial of a "soul" was involved also the denial of any system or doctrine of transmigration; there was nothing that could "transmigrate." Provision was made for the continuance of existence by a theory of re-combination of groups or constituents of being (*skandhas*). Of these every living being was composed, albeit in different proportions and degree; dissolved at death they immediately proceeded to recombine by virtue and in consequence of the force of *karma*, action with all the fruits thereof. Thus the cessation of the series of successive existences with all the misery involved in them, which was the ultimate aim, could only be achieved when the force of *karma* was entirely broken. This doctrine is of paramount importance in Buddhism, but is perhaps of later origin than the time of its founder.

NIRVANA

This state or condition of deliverance from the power

of *karma* was known as *nirvāṇa*, a restful untroubled state in which there was no more present or prospective misery or pain. It was attainable in this present life, and the Buddha himself and many of his early disciples were said to have attained it, and thenceforward they lived in peace. Their actions were performed without desire or "clinging," that is to existence, and therefore produced no fruits or consequences, which would lead to a re-combination of the *skandhas* and a renewed existence. Accordingly at death the groups fell asunder, and the individual ceased to be. *Nirvāṇa*, therefore, to Buddhist thought, never at any time connoted "annihilation." Such a conception would have been impossible with Buddhist beliefs and on Buddhist premisses. In later forms of the faith the word came to be used practically as equivalent to Paradise, a future state of felicity into which the believer might be confident of entering by the mercy of an all-powerful and compassionate deity.

Buddhism also sets forth a philosophical theory regarding the origin of evil and the mystery of suffering which is entirely materialistic. It is derived essentially from an early Indian school of thought and teaching, with contributed elements from other sources, defined and elaborated in later times. Popular as it has been in some countries and in some forms of Buddhist teaching and life, it is probably a later development, grafted upon the primitive teaching. Further or more elaborate discussion of it would here be out of place.

Christian Influence

An apparently certain and distinct Christian influence

can be traced in the Northern or Mahāyāna school of Buddhist thought and teaching. In its origin and essential elements indeed the Mahāyāna doctrine is pre-Christian and Indian. But in some of the countries at least into which Buddhism made its way—Tibet, China, and probably also, though to a less degree, Japan—it found itself in contact with Christian propaganda, and to what precise extent it is impossible to define enriched itself from the stores of Christian doctrine and practice. That the influence was mutual there is no reason to doubt. Buddhism however incurred the greater debt. For the home and strongholds of Christianity were untouched; while the foreign propaganda on Buddhist soil was necessarily and of set purpose aggressive, and had as its aim and rationale the overthrow of the opposing faith. The influence was not only doctrinal, but formal and artistic, and, as far as it is possible to judge, humane in the best sense. Much of it was overwhelmed and swept away in the changes and upheavals of later centuries. The survivals in common teaching and observance are not always easy to interpret or to allot to their respective sources; and much that is rash and unjustified has been written with regard to their mutual dependence. It must suffice here to state the general result. A consideration of the details would demand, and has often received long and not always satisfactory treatment.

Difference of the Schools: Bodhisattvas

The chief difference between the Mahāyāna and Hīnayāna systems of Buddhism lies in the speculative and mystical character of the former. Both had their origin in the north of India; and both, whether originally or in the course of time, have developed a strong theistic element, which is much more definitive and pronounced in the Northern than in the Southern school. The Hīnayāna is believed to be more true to the original teaching of Gautama. The Mahāyāna school is altogether more florid, and has elaborated an extensive system or hierarchy of gods and goddesses, for the most part derived from Indian mythology, together with a vast cosmological system, defined and graded in all its parts with the utmost precision. Some however, of the Mahāyāna sects teach a doctrine which in its singleness of aim and devotional character is hardly to be distinguished from a genuine monotheism. It is in regard to the divinities themselves, and the nature of their relation to men, that the most practically important divergence between the two schools consists. The Mahāyānist believes in the existence of an infinite number of supernatural beings, known as *Bodhisattvas*, who are not yet *Buddhas*, *i.e.* possessed of perfect knowledge and felicity, although they are destined eventually to attain to this state. Instead of immediately pursuing this course, however, in selfish indifference to the well-being or misery of mankind, they of set purpose delay their own entrance into the joy of Buddhahood, in order that they may be able to help mankind individually and collectively to secure salvation and a like blessedness. The greatest and most widely-worshipped of the Bodhisattvas is said to have taken upon him a solemn vow that he would never rest or accept for himself the joys of *nirvāṇa*, until the last of mankind had been redeemed from the woes and penalties of existence, and had entered upon a state of endless felicity. It is difficult to avoid the use of Christian phraseology in attempting to describe the Buddhist doctrine; nor do the Buddhist writers themselves escape from it. The subtle underlying difference must not be missed. In this latter case the doctrine is not necessarily or even probably borrowed.

The Hīnayāna school of belief does not teach any doctrine of this kind; nor does it recognise the existence of Bodhisattvas. In the struggle for deliverance man has no helper; each must work out his own salvation, as the Buddha himself did, by his own unaided efforts. The contrast in statement and creed is very remarkable. Mahāyānist writers maintain that this and other distinctive features of their doctrinal system were made known by the Buddha to his immediate disciples during the years that intervened between his early public ministry and his death. Of the events and teaching of these years the Buddhist books have preserved no written record. The Mahāyānist tradition is to the effect that the period was devoted to esoteric exposition with regard to the Bodhisattvas and other subjects of mystical and theological import.

The Trikāya

A further Mahāyāna doctrine of mystical significance is that involved in the conception of the triple body of the Buddha. It has been compared to the Christian doctrine of the Trinity. There is in reality little resemblance, and it is improbable that historically there has been any connection. The Buddha exists or manifests himself in a threefold form or body (*trikāya*): in the body of law or religion, which is his mystical and all-comprehensive body, the ultimate source and principle of all; the body of bliss or felicity, under which he is viewed by the deities and disembodied spirits in heaven; and the apparitional body, wherein he appears to men upon earth. The sources and history of the doctrine are almost altogether obscure. The *dharmakāya*, however, the body of the law, is the ancient Indian world-soul, the primæval and essential source of all being and the universe. In the Buddhist doctrine also the *dharmakāya* pervades and is present in all, but in its perfection is manifested only in a Buddha.

Monasticism

Buddhism also lays greater stress upon monastic rule and discipline, and attaches greater importance to the monastic life than any other religion. Gautama Buddha himself taught that only in and through the life of the monk was salvation to be gained; and but grudgingly allowed to women the formation of a corresponding order of nuns. The Mahāyāna Church has relaxed the rule; and in so doing has dignified and ennobled the laity. The Hīnayāna school, on the other hand, has remained true to the letter as it were of the constitution, and enforces, as Gautama did, the rule that only by taking upon himself the vows and observing the discipline of the monk either in the present or in some future existence can the layman secure for himself deliverance from the pains and evil of this life. The yellow robe is honoured not only theoretically but actually wherever Buddhism holds sway more than in any other lands. There is moreover some reason to believe that the early Christians and the West generally derived their knowledge of the monastic life, and the incentive towards the monastic ideal, from Buddhist example. In regard to the institution itself, however, Buddhism was not original. Hinduism had, from very ancient times, ascribed a high virtue to the solitary and ascetic habit. Gautama did not devise a new and untried manner of life; he took over a well-established and highly-honoured practice. The novelty of his teaching consisted in the stringency with which he applied and universalised the rule that only by the hard road of the monastic life was salvation to be secured. In this respect a minority of his followers only have ultimately adhered even in theory to his principles. The Buddhist layman holds now and must of necessity always have held an important place in the Buddhist community; without his generous support the monk, who may not work for his living, could not exist. But in no other great faith has the honour accorded to the monk ever included the denial to the layman of the rights and possibilities of salvation, except by the narrow way of the monkhood.

Historically therefore it is probable that the adoption of monastic principles and life throughout practically the entire religious world is due ultimately to ancient Indian practice, reinforced and carried far and wide by Buddhist missionaries. The farther these have penetrated from their source, the weaker in general has been their hold upon conscience and habit. Christian asceticism and self-repression have not equalled in intensity and persistence the Buddhist, and the latter has rarely, if at all, attained to the measure of bodily torture and effacement of bodily needs, which to its Hindu exemplar and master are commonplaces of ideal and practice. The welcome accorded to the institution, however, among so many and widely diverse peoples proves that it corresponds to a deeply-felt craving of human nature, and satisfies, if only in part, a real need of the human heart.

(3) COMPARATIVE RELIGION AND JUDAISM

The right of Judaism to a place and consideration among the great faiths of the world has often been denied. Its supposed narrowness and its undeniable aloofness have been made the grounds for refusing to it the position in the comity of religions to which its long and honourable history would seem to entitle it. And it is true that judged by mere numbers or by its present-day influence Judaism can hardly be regarded as widely powerful from a religious standpoint. Nevertheless to a science and summary of Comparative Religion its contribution is no mean one, and its importance justifies brief reference to it here. That importance may be defined as two-fold. In the first instance, doctrinal; for Judaism has borne unswerving witness to some of the most important truths on which Comparative Religion finds itself constrained to lay emphasis. Secondly, and of hardly less importance, is the permanent influence which it has exercised on some of the most widely accepted forms of religious belief. That Christianity is built upon foundations which Judaism laid is so nearly a truism that it is needless to dilate upon it. It would hardly be incorrect, however, to affirm the same of Muhammadism, so generous has been the contribution which Muhammad levied from the doctrinal system and practice of the Jews in order to frame the eclectic system which he commended to his fellow-countrymen. These two faiths at least are deeply indebted to Jewish teaching and example; and, apart from their predecessor, are historically unintelligible.

Judaism however has reacted widely, if less directly, upon other religious systems to an extent which it is difficult, perhaps impossible, absolutely to determine. The separateness of the Jews to-day and for a long time past, and the religious seclusion into which they have withdrawn, a seclusion not unwelcome to nearly all the civilised communities of the world, one which has been enforced by repression and persecution, must not lead us to withhold recognition of the missionary service which they rendered in the earlier centuries, or the success with which they maintained a doctrinal propaganda among the nations. The great truths which were their heritage, the core and essence of their religious faith, they did not isolate or keep to themselves, but with self-sacrificing diligence promulgated and taught them among other peoples. Their enemies themselves being witness, the cities of the Roman Empire were full of their converts and proselytes. These were not descendants by birth of Jewish immigrants. No doubt a certain contribution to the urban population was made from this source; in some instances it was probably considerable. With all allowance, however, for a measure of exaggeration on the part of the Roman writers, their testimony makes it certain that in the civil and religious world of their day Judaism played a large and important part. To trace entirely the ramifications of that influence is impracticable through failure of the data of evidence. Its effect may easily be underrated, and was probably more powerful and far-reaching than students of Comparative Religion have generally understood.

Monotheism

The most important and significant testimony which the Jewish nation has borne in the sphere of religious thought has been to the Divine unity and supremacy. There is one God and one only, Lord of heaven and earth, creator and ruler of all. To this monotheistic faith they have been unswervingly true, not from the beginning, but from the downfall of the Judæan kingdom and the Babylonian exile; and this is their first and chief contribution to the sum total of human belief. By the prophets of Jehovah the truth was realised and taught from the beginning. Their unceasing polemic was waged against the failure of the people to be loyal to their God, and against the folly and wickedness of the idol worship to which they had committed themselves; and it was with increasing clearness and emphasis that they set forth the character and claims of the true God. There is little evidence that by the people in general during the early centuries at least their teaching was heeded, or the doctrine they enforced received and obeyed ; it required the shock of the Exile and the destruction of their temporal kingdom to arouse the nation to a real consciousness of its national obligation and the greatness of its doctrinal heritage. Thenceforward the fidelity of the Jew to the monotheistic ideal has been as remarkable as his earlier inconsistency and refusal to listen to the exhortations and warnings of those who would have led him to a higher nobler life. Moreover with equal unanimity and conviction the prophets declared the ethical nature of the one God. His claim to worship and obedience, first from the Jew and then universally, was based not upon force or conquest but upon righteousness. It was essentially a moral claim. As such the Jews at length understood and adopted it, handed it on to their successors of other faiths, and themselves withdrawing from active proselytising or evangelistic effort, maintained a permanent and unbroken witness to a doctrine which in all its fullness had become a national possession.

Atonement

Moreover in the teaching of the later prophets at least Israel was in possession of a clear and definite preintimation of a doctrine of vicarious suffering. It was, however, in a national, not an individualistic form. The significance and obligations of vicarious endurance of hardship, distress and loss, of suffering borne not for their own sake or in their own name but for the sake of others, were set forth by some at least of the prophets with a picturesqueness and eloquence rarely equalled. How far their teaching was welcome to, or understood by their hearers or readers may be doubted. It was based upon the prophetic interpretation of the Divine covenant, whereby Israel had pledged herself to devotion and service to Jehovah. In the selfish view of prince and people alike the election by God of the nation was designed to fructify to the national security and advancement, and justified an unlimited self-confidence irrespective of fidelity or merit. The prophets on the other hand reiterate with emphasis that Jehovah's purpose in the election of the nation was not for the sake of Israel, but of the world; that the ground and basis of the covenant was mutual obligation, and that Israel's failure to observe the compact and to fulfil her part had rendered it altogether void; and that the only way in which it could be restored was the willing acceptance by Israel of a heritage of discipline, pain and even contempt, that the world might be brought to a knowledge of Jehovah and to a share in the covenant-relation to Him. The suffering however is always national, as the election and covenant are national—a chosen people for the world; and the prophets essay no interpretation or explanation of so majestic a Divine purpose.

There are suggestions of a similar doctrine in Hinduism and elsewhere. Invariably, however, in these the suffering for the sake or in the place of another is individual, not national. The prophets' doctrine was unique, and testified to a unique national self-consciousness, which perhaps did not admit of repetition under other circumstances or of development elsewhere upon the same lines. Muhammadanism stated an essentially similar doctrine with more precise definition, limiting however the scope and purpose of the redemption to its own people, and thereby retreating as it were from the breadth and liberality of the Jewish prophetic thought. In the Christian statement of belief these limitations are broken through, and a complete doctrine is enunciated which combines the universality of the prophetic teaching with the individualism imperfectly expressed already in Islām, and in some other faiths. The limitation to a nationalistic view was appropriate enough to Israel, but impossible in the wider field of the world's expanding self-consciousness and knowledge. In it, however, and in her teaching of the Divine Unity and Supremacy Israel had made no mean contribution to the store of comparative religious thought.

(4) COMPARATIVE RELIGION AND MUHAMMADANISM

Among the religions which it would not be unjust to regard as typical or representative Islām may claim a definite place, both as regards doctrine and practice. No less than Judaism it maintains and enforces a strictly monotheistic creed ; but its monotheism has adopted a character and taken on a colouring distinct from that of any other faith. Its rules also for the ordering of behaviour and life, although perhaps rivalled in strictness and detail by those of some other systems, present in their entirety features and a completeness altogether its own. For the purposes of comparative inquiry also, Muhammadism offers many advantages in its more recent origin and development. Unlike Hinduism, Buddhism, or some other older faiths it has been from the beginning in the limelight of historical knowledge and criticism. It is true that prepossession and fancy have done much to obscure its early records, and to bring into dispute details of history and progress. These, however, for the most part concern alleged matters of fact or historical reliability. The framework of creed and the inter-relation of doctrine and sect may usually be defined with certainty.

Character of Muhammad

On the character and motives of the founder himself the most contrary views have been held. On the one hand he has been regarded by his followers with a reverence scarcely inferior to that accorded to the Deity himself, his words and actions as guided unerringly by inspired wisdom, and his life as presenting the supreme pattern of justice tempered with mercy. On the other he has been assailed as the most gross of impostors, his character vilified, his principles and motives described in the darkest terms. Extreme views however have been gradually rectified, and a juster and more temperate estimate now prevails. " Perhaps few characters in history have been more complex, or have combined stronger conviction and will-power with elastic response in external matters to the influence and leading of environment. It is hardly possible to study the Qur'ān with the sanction there given to exceptional licence in the interests of the Prophet himself, and with its savage denunciations of his foes, and yet hold fast to a belief in the moral integrity and purity of Muhammad's motives and conduct. But that he at least entered upon his mission with sincerity, and a deep conviction of the wrong of idolatry, as a denial of the rights and authority of the one God, is attested by the character and devotion of his first converts and the entire history of the early years at Mecca. It must be acknowledged that it is not easy to define exactly what he did believe concerning the earlier revelations recorded in the Qur'ān. That in later years he consciously invented revelations for political and personal ends can hardly be doubted."* His greatness, however, as an organiser and leader of men, and as the originator of a profound and far-reaching religious reform, the effects of which upon the thought and belief and habit of a large proportion of mankind have been immeasurable, is not to be denied. Comparative Religion must needs endeavour to form a just estimate of the character of a man who, whatever his shortcomings, gave so permanent a form and direction to religious thought among many peoples, and founded a religious system which has endured to the present day; who has been able to win the admiration and command the allegiance of many millions of adherents throughout the known world.

His success was undeniable; and apart altogether from his own qualities and character was due in no small measure to the happiness of his opportunity. The

* *Studies in the Religions of the East*, p. 797.

last traces of overlordship or organised rule had been removed from Arabia shortly before his birth. No strong and independent system of faith or doctrine existed. That he was able, however, effectively to seize the opportunity is a testimony to the force of his nature and will. His tact and insight into the characters of other men seem never to have failed; he thoroughly understood his fellow countrymen, and knew how to utilise their services to the best advantage. And if imagination and initiative in matters of doctrine were not at his disposal he possessed the capacity nevertheless to weave together materials from many sources into an eclectic and coherent system, persuasive and simple, which commanded ready assent and has withstood the shocks of time.

In one practical respect Muhammad's foresight failed him. He made no provision for the extension of the faith beyond the limits of Arabia, or for the adaptation of its practice and the necessary modification of its demands under other conditions and among other peoples. The tradition may or may not be true that in later life he sent letters to the rulers of some foreign countries requiring their submission to Islām and to himself as the Divinely-commissioned Prophet of the faith. But the laws which he enacted for the mediæval Arabs, and the rule of creed and confession which the latter found it not difficult to accept, were to be binding for all time and under every form of society. The iron hand was laid alike upon articles of belief and upon the practical details of behaviour and life. No variation or deviation was permissible. And the liberty to modify, change or reshape in accordance with the needs of the time, the waiting upon circumstance which Muhammad claimed for himself, he denied to his adherents and successors. Islām thus presents a fixity of creed and usage, established once for all, which has been in the judgement even of its friends the greatest bar to any real progress. No other religion has so brusquely set aside local or national wont and prejudice, and compelled all to adhere to the same formula of the faith, and to bow to the same yoke of ritual observance and custom.

Mu'tazilas and Freedom of Thought

On two distinct occasions and periods in their history there have been attempts made by Musalmans themselves to secure for themselves freedom from these disabilities. The first was in the early centuries of the Abbāsid Empire by a sect or party known as *Mu'tazilas*, "separatists" or "seceders." They claimed the right in general of freedom of thought and belief, and in particular denied the orthodox doctrines of the eternity of the Qur'ān and of absolute predestination. In regard to the nature of God also they affirmed in opposition to the orthodox view that the attributes, such as hearing, sight, etc., were accidents of his eternal being, and not essential. The traditional account of their final overthrow and the triumph of rigid orthodoxy represents this as due to the ability and influence of the great scholar and teacher al-Ash'arī in the early part of the tenth century. He is said to have been an adherent of the Mu'tazilite school until his fortieth year, when with dramatic suddenness in the mosque at Basrah he proclaimed his abandonment of his former creed and return to the orthodox faith. None of the Mu'tazilite doctors were able to maintain their ground against his arguments and denunciations; and by the end of the century the sect was practically extinct.

Whatever the dialectical skill and influence of al-Ash'arī, it is certain that his conversion to orthodoxy and subsequent polemic against his former associates would not of itself have compassed the downfall of the Mu'tazila community thus abruptly, if the latter had been genuinely convinced of the rightness of their cause and prepared to make sacrifice for conscience sake. The fact appears to be that their interest lay almost entirely in mere verbal discussions and intellectual theorising. There was no strong conviction or moral force behind their argumentation, and they contended for verbal victory, not from any deep-seated love of the truth. When therefore they met their master in disputation and were vanquished in the game of splitting hairs, there was nothing left for which it seemed worth while to fight; and the collapse of the entire movement necessarily followed with little delay. Its failure is to be regretted. Had the issue been otherwise, the whole course of Muhammadan religious history would have been changed.

Modern Liberalising Movements

Under better auspices and with much brighter prospects of success the Mu'tazila revolt against the strin-

Ls. 183); E. H. परोजन् *necessity,* पराग् *Allahabad,* परांचित् *penance,* see § 144.

Note: In Pr. सलाहा (H. C. 2, 101), Skr. श्लाघा, E. H. सराह् *praise.*

186. इ *is interpolated; sometimes;* thus E. H. तिरपन् *fifty three,* Ap. Pr. * त्रिपर्ण (cf. H. C. 4, 398), Skr. त्रिपञ्चाशत्; E. H. तिरसठि *sixty three,* Ap. Pr. *त्रिसट्ठी, Skr. त्रिषष्टिः; E. H. तिरिका or त्रिका *triad,* see § 408; E. H. गिरहन् *eclipse,* Ap. Pr. ग्रहणं, Skr. ग्रहणम्; E. H. पिलही *spleen,* Pr. *पिलहिश्र, Skr. प्लीहिका; E. H. गिलानि *fatigue,* Pr. *गिलाणो (cf. H. C. 2, 106), Skr. ग्लानिः; E. H. तिरिया *woman,* Ap. Pr. *त्रिश्रा, Skr. स्त्रिका.

Note: In Pr. सिणेहो (Wb. Bh. 405. Ls. 182) or सणेहो or नेहो (H. C. 2, 102), Skr. स्नेहः, E. H. सिनेह् or सनेह् or नेह् *love;* Pr. सिरी (H. C. 2, 104), Skr. श्री, E. H. सिरि *prosperity;* Pr. किरिश्रा (H. C. 2, 104), Skr. क्रिया, E. H. किरिया *oath;* Pr. किलेसो (H. C. 2, 106) *trouble,* see § 58, note.

187. उ *is interpolated; rarely;* thus E. H. सुमिरन् or सुमरन्, *recollection,* Ap. Pr. सुमरणु (H. C. 4, 426. cf. 4, 74), Skr. स्मरणम्.

188. *The first consonant is elided; always;* thus E. H. भीतर् *within* for ब्भीतर्, A. Mg. अब्भिंतरं (§ 172), Skr. अभ्यन्तरम्; E. H. भीतै, काढै, कंगा, कंगिया, for ब्भीतै, ख्काढै, ख्कंगा, ख्कंगिया, see § 172; E. H. छमा *forgiveness* for *च्छमा, Skr. क्षमा, see §§ 36. 191; E. H. छाहै *he desires* for *च्छाहै, see § 173.

Exception. ग्य् remains, as E. H. ग्यान् *knowledge,* Skr. ज्ञानम्, see § 191; in the *khari bhásha* optionally also र् following a cons., as प्रगट् or परगट् *manifest,* § 185.

Note: In Pr. also; as a rule, see H. C. 2, 89. Vr. 3, 50; thus Pr. झाणं (H. C. 2, 26), Skr. ध्यानम्; Pr. झाश्रो or धाश्रो for *ज्झाश्रो or ड्ढाश्रो (H. C. 2, 27), Skr. ध्वजः; Pr. छमा or खमा for *च्छमा or *क्खमा (H. C. 2, 18 gives छमा in the sense of *earth* and खमा as *patience* or *forgivenes;* but in E. H., the latter does not exist, and the former means *forgiveness* or *patience*), Skr. क्षमा; Pr. ठाणं or थाणं for *ट्ठाणं or *त्थाणं (H. C. 4, 16), Skr. स्थानम्; etc.; but A. Mg. apparently has occasionally ज्झ्; as ज्झाणा° (Wb. Bh. 315. 319),

Skr. ध्यान°; or त्थूसित्ता (Wb. Bh. 295), Skr. अध्यूषित्वा, etc.; see Wb. Bh. 389. 390.

189. *The second consonant is elided;* only ह्; thus E. H. नाऊ *barber,* A. Mg. ण्हाविए or नाविए (cf. H. C. 1, 230), Skr. नापितः (or *स्नापिकः).

Note: In Pr. नेहो (H. C. 2, 102) for *ण्हेहो (not for *स्नेहो as in H. C. 2, 77), Skr. स्नेहः, E. H. नेह् *love, oil;* Pr. णिद्धं (H. C. 2, 109) for *णिह्ढं, Skr. स्निग्धम्, E. H. *deest.*

190. *अ or इ is prefixed to स् preceding any consonant; only in semitats;* thus E. H. अस्तुति or इस्तुति *praise,* Skr. स्तुतिः; E. H. अस्नान् *bathing,* Skr. स्नानम्; E. H. अस्नेह् *love,* Skr. स्नेहः; E. H. इस्तन्त्री *woman,* Skr. स्त्री; or in foreign words, as E. H. अस्कूल् or इस्कूल् *school*; E. H. इस्पंज् *sponge*; etc.

Note: A curiosity is the E. H. अचपल् *restless* for Skr. चपलः

191. *ज्ञ् and ज्ञ् become ड् and ग्य्*; only in semitats; see §§ 36. 37. In tadbh. ज्ञ् becomes ञ्; e. g., E. H. ज्ञानी or ज्ञान् *sage,* Pr. णाणी (H. C. 2, 83. Vr. 3, 5), Skr. ज्ञानी; but as a semitats. it is E. H. ग्यानी.

SECOND SECTION. ON SUFFIXES AND ROOTS.

FIRST CHAPTER. SUFFIXES.

192. The E. H. suffixes may be divided into two great classes, which I shall call the *pleonastic* and the *derivative.* The former are those, by the addition of which the meaning of a noun is not changed, thus पट् and पटा *board,* आगि and अगिया *fire,* चाम् and चमड़ा *leather,* मीठ् and मिठका *sweet,* etc. The latter are those which change the meaning of a noun. These may be subdivided into two classes; the *primary* and *secondary.* The former are those which are added to (verbal) roots and form primary bases; e. g., R. खा *eat,* खाऊ or खानिहारु *eater, glutton;* हँस् *laugh,* हँसी *laughter;* बढ् *grow,* बढ़ती *growth,* etc. The latter are added to the bases

tion and veneration of his countrymen to be eradicated, even when they seemed most sharply to conflict with a pure and spiritual monotheism. Muhammad therefore adopted these into his own system, and seems to have contented himself with endeavouring to deprive them as far as practicable of idolatrous associations. With these he combined a considerable acquaintance with and indebtedness to Judaism and Christianity, as believed and practised by communities or individuals with whom he was in touch at Medina and elsewhere. It is altogether improbable that he had any direct acquaintance with the Jewish or Christian Scriptures. Nor does the type of faith or religious life with which he came into contact seem in either case to have been of a pure or elevated character. The Judaism was debased, and the Christianity of the type that was founded upon Apocryphal Gospels and traditions, rather than that which drew its inspiration from the New Testament. He had no opportunity of knowing the best of either faith; and the numerous mistakes and inaccuracies which characterise his presentation whether of narrative or of doctrine are certainly due for the most part to imperfect information rather than to any intent to mislead. Even in the native life of Arabia itself there were traces of a purer monotheistic creed, perhaps derived ultimately from Jewish or Christian teaching, of which Muhammad was cognisant, and for which he entertained a deep respect.

Besides these Muhammad had become acquainted with Persian teaching, and a not inconsiderable element of Zoroastrian doctrine was thereby introduced into his system. The contribution was rather cosmological and eschatogical than doctrinal in the formal sense. Especially in regard to eschatology and the future life Muhammad appears to have been attracted by Persian conceptions, and to have founded his teaching almost altogether upon a Persian basis.

The eclectic system of doctrine, therefore, which is thus set forth as the product of experience and thought during many years does not present its author as a profound or original thinker. Muhammad was not a great student or theologian. There cannot, however, be denied to him the credit of skill and insight in the weaving together of the whole, and judged by results his work has stood thus far the test of time, and has approved itself to the consciousness and thought of very many peoples. It is true also that the strength of Islām has been like that of its founder in organisation and enthusiasm for a name and cause, rather than in persuasiveness and the niceties of doctrinal definition or belief; and that for whatever it has achieved in the regulation of faith and the imposition of a creed it has been indebted for the most part to external influence and thought working on a mind unusually plastic and open to impressions from without, and to historical opportunity and circumstance which favoured the Prophet himself, and which in the early expansion of Islām brought it into touch with the most varied culture and civilisations.

PERSIAN INFLUENCE

The most powerful influence subsequent to the death

of Muhammad was that of Persian civilisation and thought. A second and scarcely inferior place in the ultimate issue should be assigned to the science and philosophy of Greece. In the middle ages Muhammadan scholars eagerly translated and assimilated the writings of Greek authorities and teachers in almost every branch of learning. Persia, however, partly because of its proximity to the sources and centre of Muhammadan rule, played a more dominant rôle in the early centuries of Muhammadan history. Many of the Abbāsid rulers, and the court of Baghdad almost exclusively were under the sway of Persian manners and tradition. Persian ministries controlled the government. It was Persian scholars who communicated to an otherwise illiterate people their love of letters and eager interest in science. Although overrun and conquered by Muslim soldiers the land was never really "Islāmised." It accepted a political yoke which it was not strong enough to reject, and while adopting a formula of faith and rendering outward obedience remained essentially heterodox. The Persians, though nominally Muhammadans, have always maintained a certain measure of freedom of thought, and been ready to accommodate themselves to heretical views.

Shi'ahs

A further dominating influence on Persian thought and religious development, although not on that people alone, has been attachment, almost fanatic in its intensity, to the house of 'Alī the son-in-law of the Prophet. The strength of the Shī'ah sect is in Persia; and though the numbers of the sect are small compared with those of the orthodox Sunnīs, the significance of their creed is great. Affection for the family of Alī and loyalty to the claims of his descendants were stimulated to a unique degree by the "murder" of Husain, his son, at Karbalā in the year A.D. 680. His death is in effect regarded by all Shī'ahs as the greatest example of self-sacrifice and an atonement for sin. Muhammad is reported to have foretold his martyrdom: "He will die for the sake of my people." And Husain also, before undertaking the expedition which ended so disastrously, is said to have rejected the counsel of his friends to consult his own safety with the words: "How can I forget my people, seeing that I am about to offer myself for their sakes." The battle, or massacre of Karbalā took place on the tenth of Muharram, the first month of the Muhammadan (lunar) year; and the anniversary of the death of Husain is celebrated by all Shī'ahs in the Muharram festival and ceremonies, wherein his "martyrdom" is commemorated, and the bitter feelings of indignation and resentment which it caused are kept alive to this day. Thus Islām also, if only in a secondary degree and under an unorthodox form, testifies to the longing of the human heart for an atonement.

TRADITION

Muhammadan teaching assigns to "tradition," duly authenticated and accepted, as important a place and function as did the Jewish doctors of the early centuries. The observance of the *Sunnat*, the "usage" or "rule" of the faith, the second of the four foundations of Muhammadan doctrine and law, is said to have been enjoined by Muhammad himself. It consists of a very large number of traditional sayings and directions of the Prophet, handed down originally by word of mouth, criticised and subjected to tests of authenticity by scholars, and finally after sifting committed to writing in six orthodox books, which hold practically the same position in Muhammadanism as the Talmud among the Jews. The six books however are not recognised by the Shī'ahs, who have five different collections of their own. Ultimately these, together with later rulings and judgements were crystallized or codified in the four great systems of Muhammadan jurisprudence, to one or other of which every Sunnī Muslim attaches himself. They were founded by Muhammadan doctors of great eminence in the eighth and ninth centuries. The schools are at variance, however, only to a very slight extent in legal and doctrinal matters. The discussions which were held turned mainly upon the rights of private judgement in the valuation of the traditions and in a broader sense of the observances of religion in general.

Together with the Qur'ān and the Sunnat an equal authority at least theoretically in determining the rules and principles of the Muhammadan faith attached to *Ijmā'*, "unanimity" or "agreement," and *Qiyās* "analogy." By the former are intended legal decisions or judgements promulgated by one of the "Companions of the Prophets" or an early doctor of repute; they were then generally accepted, and became part of legal usage and observance. Later teachers, however learned, were not supposed to have the authority or right thus to formulate decisions of law. *Qiyās*, on the other hand, provides for cases that may arise to which no existing rule directly applies, but which are sufficiently similar to others to enable them to be determined by precedent or analogy. On these four "foundations" Muhammadan creed and practice are based.

The Kalimah

It is not a little remarkable also that in Islām doctrine and observance are placed upon the same footing, and are regarded, theoretically at least, as equally necessary to salvation. A similar correlating of demands that in reality belong to entirely different spheres may be noted in other religions, but hardly so confidently or to so great an extent as in Muhammadism. To go on pilgrimage to Mecca is, in theory at least, as important and essential to salvation as to believe in one God or in Muhammad as his Prophet. The latter primary article of faith is the so-called *kalimah* or creed, the recital of which constitutes a man a Muslim and believer, the denial a *kāfir* or infidel. Undoubtedly the simplicity of this requirement has been one of the factors that has contributed most materially to the success of Muhammadanism among backward and primitive tribes. There have been many others, political and social, varying according to the constitution of the people and the nature of their country. But as compared with the elaborate explanations and long apprenticeship which most religions demand as a condition precedent to admission to full rights and fellowship, Islām begins its proselytising and missionary work with a very considerable initial advantage. By the recital of a plain and simple formula the transition from any other religion or none at all to the full status of a believer is at once accomplished; and the profitable results both social and economic that accrue from the change are often of much value even in countries that would usually be regarded as not uncivilised.

Theology

The Muhammadan conception of the one God, as elucidated and expounded by the Muhammadan doctors themselves, presents several features of interest and is set forth at length in treatises on Muslim theology. There are seven Attributes, namely, Life, Knowledge, Power, Will, Hearing, Vision, and Speech, the nature and relation of which were discussed in great detail and with much learning. In particular the Mu'tazilas denied the eternity of the Attributes, and in this respect again found themselves at variance with the opinion of the orthodox. The most important and commanding feature in the Divine character is absolute and irresponsible power, controlled by no moral considerations and mitigated by no feelings of pity or regard. Hence the Muslim is a fatalist in the most pronounced and absolute meaning of the word. The Divine will is irresistible, and has decreed in every detail the entire course of the universe which He governs, and the fate each moment of every creature therein. It is useless therefore to contend with God, who determines good or evil as He wills. The only attitude possible for man is that of complete and passive resignation. Thus in carrying to its logical conclusion the belief in a God of supreme power and irresistible controlling will Islām takes precedence of all other religions. Its dogma of predestination and of fate is based upon its conception of the Divine nature, and only makes explicit what is implicitly contained therein. The Divine government is in the last resort executive of the Divine decrees; and leaves no room for human free-will, forethought or choice.

Muslim Protestant Movement

It was inevitable that the Mu'tazila revolt against a dogma which negatives and destroys human liberty, when revived as it has been within the last half-century under the influence of Western civilisation and thought, should take strong root and spread rapidly among the educated classes in all lands. The Muslim clergy with the colleges and schools under their control have been hitherto the stronghold of conservatism and orthodoxy. The movement is reported to be gathering strength and momentum even among these; and the ancient University of Al-Azhar at Cairo, whose influence is unrivalled in the Muhammadan world, has modified its traditional curriculum to admit new subjects and alien methods of training and the strange light of modern thought.

Comparative Doctrine and Practice

These are the doctrines most characteristic of Islām, in which a comparison with other religions is most instructive. Muhammadan teaching however on other subjects is often distinctive, and contrasts more or less strongly with the beliefs or practices of other peoples. Thus while their eschatology is borrowed for the most part from Persia, there is super-added to it the dogma of the final salvation of all Muhammadans, irrespective of character or desert, and the hopeless ruin and perdition of all unbelievers. The legal rules for almsgiving, which prescribe that a certain fixed proportion of property and income shall be devoted to the service of God and the relief of need, are perhaps derived in part from the same source ; but for the conception in general and probably for most of its detailed working, Muhammad seems to have been indebted to Jewish example and practice. The rites of the pilgrimage and the legal and religious obligations with which it was supported are of native Arabian origin, and of considerable but unknown antiquity. Muhammad incorporated these into his religious system and made them obligatory, modifying them as far as he was able to do in a monotheistic sense, but retaining many practices of a superstitious and polytheistic nature with which apparently he was unable to dispense, finding them too deeply rooted in the affections of the people. Finally the conception of prayer which Islām inculcates and fosters is distinct from that of Judaism or Christianity, or indeed that of any of the great religions, all of which attach a spiritual meaning and significance to the practice. In Islām prayer is essentially a repetition of set phrases, accompanied by ordered movements of the body and genuflexions. The phrases used are ascriptions of praise or declarations of the Divine nature or majesty, and are entirely wanting in the element of petition. There is no initiative on the part of the worshipper, or of the *imām* or leader of the prayers, except in so far as permissible variations in the order or number of the sentences employed may be regarded as such. It is therefore essentially mechanical, and the element of spontaneity so highly valued in many faiths and regarded as of the essence of true prayer is altogether absent. Here also, however, the new spirit has sometimes found expression, and under the influence of modern thought, intercourse and environment, Muhammadan meetings for prayer have adopted a tone and meaning more real and spiritual than anything enjoined by the founder or followed in the practice of the centuries.

Mysticism

The Muhammadan sects of Sunnīs and Shī'ahs have sometimes been compared to the Greek and Roman Churches in Christendom. There is in reality little parallelism or similarity between them. The leading distinctive tenets of the Shī'ahs, the belief in the divine right of Alī and his sons, and the doctrine of the Imām, rest upon a mystical basis, and have little or nothing in common with Western beliefs. To this last term, and also to some other religious titles, Sunnī usage assigns an altogether different connotation. Shī'ah thought and creed is indeed fundamentally mystical. Historically its home has always been in Persia, and the greater number of its adherents are Persians. And it was within the Shī'ah sect or church that the mystical Sūfī movement found a home and congenial sphere, whose various developments have so deeply influenced the Muhammadan world. Sūfī doctrines are essentially the same as those of mystics universally. They believe in the supreme and unerring guidance of the Inner Light, follow the prescribed path which leads in ecstasy and love to complete union with the Divine, and adopt and teach pantheistic views of the universe and of God; the latter is the sole reality in the universe, and the world therefore with all that it contains is unreal and an illusion. Nor did the Sūfī leaders themselves hesitate to draw the conclusion that ultimately moral responsibility and obligation were non-existent, for God was the final author of all conduct and action. Almost the whole of Persian poetry is Sūfiistic. From the same source also were derived the numerous and powerful Darwish (dervish) orders in Islām, which are all deeply interpenetrated by mystical principles and thought.

The essential doctrines of Sūfiism are of course of far greater antiquity than the rise of Islām. Nearer and further Asia had been familiar with them for many centuries. Greek and Alexandrian Neo-Platonism and the Hindu Vedānta in the West and East respectively had been the most powerful and influential exponents of doctrines in their most important features essentially the same as those which the Sūfī doctors adopted and promulgated. Accordingly it has frequently been maintained that the origin and rise of Sūfiism are to be ascribed to one or other of these, or to both combined. There is nothing improbable in either of these hypotheses, and perhaps the Indian theory has most in its favour. It is at least equally possible however that the movement was in its beginnings really and entirely indigenous, similar forces and tendencies manifesting themselves in similar results. In later times contact and communication took place in many directions, and the borrowing and assimilation were probably not alone on one side. It is impossible, however, in the absence of historical data and evidence, to work out any satisfactory or convincing scheme of inter-relation.

Religious Compromise

Brief reference should be made also to that which is among the least commendable features of the Shī'ah faith. It is difficult to be certain how far it is actually put into practice. No other great religion, however, so openly professes and defends dissimulation. According to the Shī'ah doctrine of religious compromise or reserve, it is at all times permissible for a believer to conceal or disavow his true faith, or even to represent himself as an inquirer into or adherent of another religious system, if confession of his own faith would subject him to peril or even inconvenience of any kind. It is asserted that this maxim was persistently acted upon in the early history of the Bābī movement, and by Mīrzā 'Alī Muhammad, the Bāb, himself. It has certainly been one of the chief obstacles in the way of obtaining accurate information concerning its progress. And there can be little doubt that the Bahāīs habitually practise it in their communications with the followers of other religions, whom they seek to win over or to persuade of the excellence of their own faith.

Missions.

Islām has always given itself over in a very high degree to missionary endeavour and proselytism. If its efforts had been conducted uniformly by methods of persuasion alone and with an absence of compulsion or force, the zeal with which the interests of extension and propagandism were and are being served could have won nothing but commendation. Unfortunately this has not been so, especially in the early stages of rapid advance and conquest. Attempts to deny or explain away the instances of enforced conversion to Islām, or to interpret in a milder sense the injunction of the Prophet himself of the use of the sword in overcoming unbelief (Qur. ii. 245, viii. 40, ix. 5) have failed to carry conviction. Few churches however can afford to throw many stones; perhaps Buddhism alone is blameless in this respect. This missionary work is being continued at the present day, and in districts of Africa and elsewhere meets with much success. There is little or no organisation or system employed, no statistics are compiled, or reports issued. To a considerable extent the work is in the hands of the Darwīsh orders, especially the Sanūsīyah in North Africa and the Sudan, whose itinerant preachers travel far and wide. Independent teachers also and leaders are often indefatigable in their zeal, and gather around them large bands of disciples. With the exception of Christianity Muhammadanism may be said to be the only religion that is now actively missionary to any marked extent; the rivalry in this respect between the two faiths is likely to increase rather than diminish. The missionary zeal of Buddhism has for many centuries been altogether in abeyance. The partial and local revival at the present time seems almost wholly forced and artificial, stimulated perhaps rather by emulation and example than by any real interest in or desire for the extension of the faith.

(5) COMPARATIVE RELIGION AND CHRISTIANITY

There is the less need to enter upon any discussion at length of the leading doctrines of Christianity in their relation to the science of Comparative Religion in that many references of likeness and contrast will be found in the preceding pages. It will be well, however, briefly to summarise, and formally to present in order some of the chief points for consideration. A theory of Comparative Religion that omitted to take account of Christianity, or regarded its relation to other faiths and its contribution to the sum total of human belief as a side-issue or negligible, would be self-convicted of ignoring that which judged by any standard has been the greatest religious factor in the history of the human race. This fact itself, of pre-eminent diffusion and influence, requires to be accounted for, its conditions and causes reasonably set forth. It is too often ignored by those who explain away or deny the veracity of the traditional accounts of the Christian origins; it is neither reasonable nor scientific to criticise the origins as it were by themselves without taking into consideration the before and after. To many minds the fact of Christianity together with its power and present position in the world is the strongest argument for the substantial truth of the records of its birth and earlier developments.

Principles and Present Position

The adherents of Christianity, including both the Greek and Roman Churches, numerically exceed to a considerable extent those of any other religion. This has perhaps been true only within the last century; but the preponderance is growing, and appears likely yet more to increase. It is true also, with of course some notable exceptions, of which the Japanese will probably be regarded as the most striking and admirable, that the nations that have led the advance in all directions of progress, in science, in literature, in general enlightenment, and also in the modern reform of principles and manners, have been the Christian. It will freely be acknowledged that there has been in the past much blindness and stagnation among peoples professedly Christian; and prejudice and obscurantism have suffered their just penalty in the decay of civil and political power, in social and economic retrogression and the loss of name and repute. On the whole however, the Christian peoples have stood for progress and liberal thought, have been foremost in enterprise and the arts, and inferior to none in scientific achievement and in all that makes for greatness and nobility whether of conduct or of character. Judged by results alone the Christian faith may and ought to enter upon a comparison with other religions without any reservation and with nothing to fear. To adopt any other attitude, or to shrink from the test would be a confession of inferiority; it would appear to betray self-consciousness of inefficiency or inability with the great heritage of the past to meet the greater demands of the present and the future; and would justly be visited in the minds of many fair-thinking men with the strongest possible condemnation.

The doctrines which it is most pertinent to consider are those of the nature and being of God, of the nature and destiny of the soul together with the mode and method of its redemption, and of sin.

Theology

In its general characteristics the Christian conception of God has been described as *anthropocentric* or *theanthropic*. All conceptions that the human mind forms are of course necessarily anthropocentric in the wider sense; thought cannot do otherwise than utilise the experiences of the thinker, and frame its ideas on accepted models. What is intended in the definition is rather to suggest a contrast with *theocratic*, as two varying and more or less opposed types of thought concerning the Divine attributes and character. The latter lays stress upon the sovereignty and supremacy of God. He rules, and man cannot do otherwise than submit to His ruling; the worshipper is a servant or slave, who may not discuss or dispute his Master's will, but only obey. There is little or nothing in common between the divine and human natures, the barrier between man and God tends to become more arduous to surmount, and no real apprehension on man's side or mutual communion is practicable. This seems to be essentially an Oriental view, and is framed upon an Oriental conception of the character and relationships of a well-known type of Oriental despot. Actually, however, it is exhibited most completely in the Jewish and Muhammadan faiths, more especially in the latter, where the theocratic nature of the Supreme God is distinctively assumed and taught. The theanthropic idea is more widely diffused, alike in the East and in the West, and makes a more powerful appeal to human nature and the craving for personal sympathy. The deity is conceived in the likeness of man, with human qualities and passions, influenced by similar motives, and prompted to action by similar causes. Illustrations may be found among the Greeks, the peoples of India, the European nations generally, and in almost every part of the ancient or modern world.

To a theanthropic range of ideas alone belong the doctrines of the Fatherhood of God, or of the Incarnation. Either would be in the utmost degree abhorrent from the theocratic point of view; it would suggest a degradation of the Divine Being, the mere thought of which would be displeasing, as it is to the Muhammadan. Similarly, a belief in the deification of man or his final union with God can find no place in a creed constructed on a theocratic basis. On the other hand, by races or peoples whose thought of God is theanthropic, hardly any conception is in one form or another more widely received and welcomed. The difference in the mode of apprehension is not seldom reflected in the titles given to the Divine Being, or the personal names which children receive at their birth. "Zeus the father of Gods and men," Dyauspitar, Jupiter, Wodan, will serve as examples as the one hand; Allah, Shaddai, and the sacred name among the Jews which in English is expressed as Jehovah, will exemplify the other tendency. Devadatta, Theodorus, etc., are Indian and Greek names which with many others give expression to the parents' sense of immediate indebtedness to a beneficent and interested god. In earlier Judaistic thought there existed a considerable theanthropic element, reflected in the strongly-marked anthropomorphism of the patriarchal and other narratives of the Pentateuch, and derived probably from Babylon and Egypt. In the later history and development of the national life may be traced the gradual stiffening of thought into the theocratic conception of the Divine, which becomes almost exclusively the accepted doctrine of later Judaism. There have always been Jewish leaders and teachers, however, who have contended for the rival view, more natural, satisfying and tender as it appeared to be, and more adapted to meet human craving and need. Islām from the beginning has presented the most stringent and complete example of the theocratic mood. And essentially the same tendency may be traced in the Hīnayāna school of Buddhism.

It is almost superfluous to point out that there are dangers to true belief on either side; that neither view is complete in itself or free from difficulty. The limitations of human thought, finding itself compelled to express itself in terms of human experience and analogy, are manifest on every hand. The rival doctrines of God are neither mutually complementary and thus in association to be regarded as adequate to the need, nor on the other hand are they wholly antagonistic. In actual fact they have often been blended, as in primitive Hebrew teaching, in the hope that thus a satisfying definition or conception of the Divine nature or being might be evolved. The hope has never justified itself; and as a secondary, although not the immediate aim of the science of Comparative Religion, its attainment seems as far off as ever. All attempts to find a compromise or practical *via media* have fallen short of success; and it is obvious that there are elements and qualities in the Divine which do not lend themselves to classification under either of these two heads. Of these the chief perhaps are those ideas and relations which are usually termed metaphysical, which have been material for inquiry and argument in many, perhaps all, religions.

In the Christian formula or creed the endeavour to meet the requirements of both conceptions of the Divine character is seen at its best, and has achieved probably the largest degree of success that is possible. Without labouring a distinction which did not appear essential, and for which human history seemed to afford sufficient justification and parallel, Christianity taught with emphasis the doctrines both of the overlordship and of the fatherhood of God. The latter was on the whole represented as the most important and characteristic doctrine; so much so that in some forms of Christian teaching it has obscured to a dangerous extent the complementary and essential doctrine of the Divine supreme rule. The definite assertion in Christian teaching of the Divine Fatherhood has been described as unique, and regarded as constituting the ground of its indefeasible claim to universal hearing and acceptance. In India and Greece however, and among many other peoples also, this doctrine was more or less clearly realised, and its consequences thought out and proclaimed. It is true that in Christendom a greater prominence was assigned to it, both in the original teaching of the Founder, and in the estimate of the Church itself and in its missionary propaganda. The doctrine of the Divine sovereignty, however, was not obscured, its rights were fully maintained and jealously guarded, while its difficulties especially in regard to human competence and free-will were more fully than elsewhere realised, and a solution of the problem of reconciliation sought. The tendency of modern Christian thinking seems to lie on the one hand in the direction of recognising more frankly and fully the necessarily anthropomorphic character of the former aspect of the theological doctrine, and the inadequacy of the parallels drawn from human parenthood; and on the other of a more clear comprehension of the fact that the distance to which the latter relegates the Divine, and the separateness of sphere and function which it postulates, form a real bar to communion and the satisfaction of the religious instincts and cravings of the human heart. Whatever theory or formula may ultimately be adopted as expressing in the best manner possible under the limitations of human thought and language the truth concerning the Divine nature and being, the subject will always be among the most important to which the science of Comparative Religion is under obligation to address itself.

Immortality of the Soul

Christianity has consistently taught the doctrine of the immortality of the soul, a heritage in large part at least from a system or systems of teaching anterior to her own. Difficulties, however, have always been encountered by the exponents of her doctrine in the attempt to define clearly either the nature of the soul itself, or the meaning of the predicate of immortality. The crude conception of a material soul, less material perhaps than the body, but still of similar substance to that of the visible tangible universe around, has long been abandoned. A similar theory of the soul's nature has been formulated in many other religious systems, and to some of these in all probability Christianity was indebted for the idea. A refuge was found in a definition purely negative, that the soul was "immaterial." A similar negative connotation was originally all that was implied in the assertion of the soul's immortality, namely, that it was not mortal, not subject to death or dissolution. In this form it is a practically universal article of belief among all peoples, primitive or highly civilised; and where the doctrine of transmigration is accepted and taught it is this quality or characteristic of the soul that receives the emphasis. In the Christian teaching, however, the expression is more than a mere negation of mortality, and takes on the positive or semi-positive connotation of eternal or everlasting. It is usually conceived as predicating certain positive qualities or endowments, as ethereality, continuity of consciousness, etc. In the stress laid upon these associated or adventitious ideas Christianity is not alone among the great religious systems, but has perhaps made them a larger part of her doctrine of a future life. Essentially, however, and in the final analysis the conception is negative, and denies the participation of the soul in those qualities or issues which are denoted by the term "mortal"; and it is upon this fundamental aspect that systems in which philosophical or metaphysical conceptions predominate have insisted. From the conception of the future condition or fate of the soul "mortal" limitations or attributes are eliminated; and to the new life which has survived death the Christian creed and Christian thought refuse logically and consistently to assign any definite term or end.

Anthropomorphic and Dualistic Conceptions

Few other religious systems have attempted to make positive statements or definitions on these subjects. Where such exist, they are usually vague and elusive, or anthropomorphic as in primitive forms of faith. More or less definite traces of anthropomorphism of this character may be found in the teaching even of the more advanced religions. It is most fully developed and remarkable perhaps among the ancient Egyptians.

The soul in the form of a bird hovers over and near the resting-place of the body. This same conception is met with not seldom elsewhere. The bird which is capable of sustaining itself in the air is regarded a a fit emblem of the soul which rises at death from the corpse. A doctrine of the future life, conceived in less materialistic and more positive terms, assumes usually one or other of two forms. It either maintains the identity of the soul with God, a doctrine which issues in pantheism and was carried to its extreme and logical conclusion in the Indian Vedānta ; or asserting their distinct and separate individuality it is involved in a more or less pronounced dualism of the Divine and human. Dualistic theories of this nature have no relation to a doctrine of the essential and perpetual conflict of world-powers or principles, good and evil, as the term is perhaps usually understood. There is no contrast or opposition ; rather a drawing together of those who nevertheless remain two and not one. There is however considerable variety in the precise forms which the doctrine assumes.

Eschatology

The final consummation or end which in general these theories contemplate is usually described as "absorption," a union of the soul with God, in which the individuality, and therewith the personal consciousness of the former is lost. Certain types of the theory, among which are to be found some of the more spiritual and effective faiths of India, endeavour to conserve the individuality of the human soul while strenuously maintaining as its goal ultimate and entire oneness with the Divine. The difficulty recurs, however, and is never completely overcome, of conceiving or explaining a permanent duality of consciousness, which is at the same time essentially and irrevocably one. In most instances also an immortality of pre-existence is affirmed, and in this case the destiny of the soul is described as a "return" into the bosom or substance of the Eternal, whence in the beginning it came forth. Logically it was found to be as difficult or impossible to predicate a real beginning as to mark off or define an end. Both alike were posited as it were arbitrarily; and there appeared to be no reason or obvious ground for the selection of one limiting era or state rather than another. Hinduism ultimately preferred to formulate a theory of transmigration, more far-reaching and complete than has elsewhere been known; which appeared indeed to satisfy the claims of a just retribution, but at the same time accentuated the difficulty of finding a reasonable ground either for a beginning or an end of the *saṁsāra*, or cycle of existence. In Indian terminology this was known not as re-incarnation, but as "renewed" or "recurrent death." The *saṁsāra* came to a close, when the death was final, not necessarily as regarded the individual existence, but as far as further sojourn upon earth in another body was concerned. With theories of transmigration, however carefully formulated and guarded, Christianity alone among the great religions, with the exception of the nearly-related systems of Judaism and Muhammadanism, has consistently refused to have anything to do. There are probably traces of it however to be found in ancient Jewish belief.

With these somewhat important exceptions therefore the Indian doctrine of the future has closer affinities to the Christian than perhaps is shown by any other faith. Historically the former has been developed from two differing conceptions, originally independent, which apparently for some considerable period existed side by side, and ultimately endeavoured to establish a mutual compromise. This was only successful to the extent that the theory which finally prevailed, that of transmigration, borrowed features from its rival. The latter taught that recompense for the deeds of the present life was awarded not in a renewed life upon earth which followed immediately upon the earlier, but in an existence of felicity or woe in another world. The common element as it were of the two theories was the exact fruition of all the actions of this life in a future determined in all respects and automatically by their character and worth. In the theistic faiths redemption was by the grace of God, through His infinite pity for the sinful and suffering sons of men. The Māhāyana school of Buddhism expressed the same belief, departing therein from primitive Buddhist doctrine as set forth in its sacred books, that by the immeasurable grace and compassion of Amida all men, whatever their faults, might obtain salvation. Thus these sects, the Vaishnavite in India and the Buddhist Mahāyāna in China and Japan might not unfairly be termed the evangelical Churches of the East. The ordered Christian doctrine, however, marks an advance upon these in the stress it lays upon ethical requirements. Salvation is by the grace of the Divine, but by a grace that is mindful of moral conditions and requires proof of moral purpose and amendment. In other respects also the Christian theory is more elaborate, makes more pertinent and wider demands on the human side, and has sought to work out more completely the significance and possibilities of its teaching as it bears upon the conception of the Divine nature and will.

Redemption

The Indian philosophical theory of redemption by knowledge has no counterpart in Christian thought. As a higher esoteric doctrine of release from the pains and penalties of the earthly life it is contrasted with a doctrine of salvation by works. The former ensures more certainly and effectively the desired result, but is available only for those of loftier spiritual insight and capacity; ordinary men must pursue the path of deliverance through works and accumulate merit for themselves by righteous deeds. The enlightened man may dispense with adventitious merit of this sort. The knowledge intended however is not science or wisdom in general, but knowledge of a definite fact, namely the identity of the human soul with the divine. He who realises this is *ipso facto* delivered from the bonds and miseries of existence and the fatal consequences of action. The philosophical knowledge therefore which brings salvation is of a different nature entirely from that presupposed by any doctrine of redemption by grace. Deliverance is not a change of status or character but the realisation of a fact. This fact more-over is not new, or in any way emergent from previous conditions. It has always been as it is at the moment, but ignorance has concealed it from the mind. Know-ledge removes the veil, and makes the truth evident. The practical effect of the doctrine, which is widely accepted in India, has not been great. It has been received as a philosophical theory, but has perhaps necessarily exercised little influence on experience or life.

Islām teaches that redemption is by the irresponsible will and fiat of the Supreme. Allah has determined the final salvation of all Muhammadans, the hopeless ruin and perdition of all unbelievers. His purpose is definite and fixed; and nothing that man can do can in any way change or modify the decrees of fate. The Muham-madan therefore is a fatalist, and consistently carries the same principle and conviction into all the walks of life. Similar theories of destiny have proved attractive at all times to certain types of mind, in ancient Greece and Rome as well as in India, and have more or less controlled no inconsiderable part of Christian Protestant thought. In Islām, however, the doctrine has been more fully accepted and put into practice as a rule of life than in any other creed. It finds itself always in conflict with what appears to be sufficient and irrefutable evidence of human free-will and self-deter-mination. And except among Muhammadans the theory has shown in recent years considerable and apparently increasing diminution of influence on belief and conduct.

SIN

Finally, in its conception of sin and its teaching with regard to it Christianity differs widely from most other forms of faith, and has created and fostered a conscience in this respect, which will for the most part be sought in vain amongst non-Christian peoples. So universally is this the case, that where similarity of idea or thought is traced, the hypothesis of a definite borrowing from Christian sources has usually been advanced. This is not always the fact, although in many instances it is historically probable; in the two most important and striking examples of certain forms of Hindu and Buddhist belief it is not likely that in the first instance there was either contact or mutual influence. In the later history and development of these creeds, however, Christian influence is unmistakable, and it is probable that the original conception of sin was among the articles of their faith which underwent in consequence considerable modification. It is not possible, however, to trace with precision the circumstances under which borrowing took place, or except in the most general way to define the place or time. For many centuries Hinduism and Christianity have been working in juxtaposition in India; and a similar contact and rivalry took place between Buddhist and Christian teaching in the early centuries of our era, certainly in Northern India and Tibet and probably over a large part of the continent of Asia. With these important exceptions, in primitive thought and in the earlier stages of religious evolution in general sin as violation of a Divine precept or law does not connote moral guilt.

The law is not ethical, nor does it concern itself with wrongdoing in an ethical sense. It prescribes ritual and regulates the mode or modes of outward observance in approaching the gods; and righteousness is essentially the keeping of the rules, sin their violation or neglect.

A people thus taught and trained will have no sense of sin as involving a moral element of behaviour or conscience. A very considerable part of the ancient Mosaic law is constituted on these lines. Christianity is almost alone among ancient religions in the stress which it lays upon the ethical character of wrongdoing, and the emphasis and completeness with which it defines sin as moral transgression. The thought appears in the Old Testament, especially in the Psalter; and a not inconsiderable part of the literature of ancient Babylon gives touching and eloquent expression to the same idea. Christianity also stands almost alone in its entire abandonment of the ritualistic conception. Even with those sects which attach most importance to the external form, the failure to observe this is not "sin" in the strict sense of the term. "Sin" is violation of a moral law, whose source is the Divine will, and which finds its sanction in the educated human consciousness of ethical right and wrong. It is evident that doctrine of this character is not without its dangers, especially where the moral consciousness is to any extent immature or enfeebled. It has in fact issued in antinomian abuses. Mystical theories of every kind are by their nature liable to proceed to these extremes, and the unfortunate results thereof are sufficiently illustrated in the history of Christianity and other faiths.

PART III

ACHIEVEMENTS AND PROSPECTS

It is evident therefore that the study of the science of Comparative Religion, and the new outlook which it has opened up into the principles and practice of the religious life, have raised many questions of vital interest and significance, and in some instances at least have given larger form and definition to outstanding problems of religion and theology, the full solution of which can hardly be said to be yet within sight. The importance of the subjects with which the science is concerned and of the issues which it presents for consideration can hardly be exaggerated. They are momentous in the first degree because they affect man's spiritual origin and destiny, and are ultimately resolvable not in material terms, but in terms of the immaterial and supernatural. They are questions moreover upon which men differ most widely, feel most deeply, and often appear most irreconcilably opposed in conviction and judgement. The experience of students has been illuminating in this respect. The brief history of the science is strewn with discarded theories which more or less confidently formulated have been based upon a very limited induction, and have proved to be in conflict with whole orders and tracts of belief and fact of which their authors were apparently unconscious. And once again it has been demonstrated that the convictions and prejudices (*praejudicia*, in the literal sense), which belong to the sphere of religion, are those by which men in general are most deeply stirred, and which they are most passionately concerned to defend.

It has been urged moreover against Comparative Religion, and in deprecation of its claims to a hearing, that the results of its work hitherto have been almost entirely destructive. Of unsettlement and the weakening or overthrow of existing theories or beliefs there has been much, but of constructive achievement that has stood or is likely to stand the test of criticism very little. The charge has been made in all seriousness; and upon it has sometimes been based the definite refusal to concede recognition to the new science or a position of equality among the better established orders of knowledge. It is not difficult to furnish an adequate refutation or reply. It is true that apart from general and for the most part unsatisfactory theorising little has been attempted in the way of constructive work. The time for such work is not yet, the science is young, its data are incomplete, the workers are few, their efforts are largely unco-ordinated, and the field to be investigated and the harvest of fact to be garnered is almost limitless. It is rather a matter of congratulation that so much has been done than of reproach that so much more has been left undone. The services moreover which the science of Comparative Religion may with confidence hope to render to the cause of truth have been more clearly defined, and indications have been given of the lines of progress and research whereby assured results will be attained. And further, it has been no light or inconsiderable achievement that already the workers of many countries and nations have been drawn together in a mutual understanding and sympathy, that is full of promise for the future.

The most important issue raised is not that of the worth and truth of religion itself, as a fact or factor in human life. That has been amply established and vindicated, no less than its universality. But of the measure and proportion of truth which may be found in any given system or profession of faith—in *a* religion, distinguished as a definite concrete system or collection of beliefs and observances from religion in general; whether the mind of man may be conceived in any instance to have built up a structure of religious belief which is wholly unsubstantial, or whether it may be asserted of every form of religious faith that has won the heart and commanded the allegiance of mankind that it contains an element, however limited or overgrown with error it may be, of reality and truth. In this respect the science of Comparative Religion, young as it is among the sciences and still feeling its way, has responded with no uncertain sound. In all faiths there may be recognised a searching after truth, which has not been wholly disappointed of success. The most elementary and degraded systems of belief, that can hardly lay claim to the title of a system, but are little more than a loosely joined assemblage of ideas with regard to the supernatural, are not wholly and absolutely mistaken and false, the darkness is not a darkness without the promise of a dawn. So far, Comparative Religion has interpreted and vindicated the Christian belief that God has not left Himself without a witness in the hearts of men. If it were otherwise Comparative Religion, which, like the other sciences, has as its ultimate aim the establishment of the truth, would be deprived in large part of its *raison d'être*. It might enforce a contrast between the virtue of the one and the vice of the other, but no real or fruitful comparison would be practicable. To sift the right thought from the erring and mistaken, to form an estimate of the measure of the former in the various faiths of the world, and to establish a standard, are tasks already essayed and in part accomplished, but far as yet from their complete realisation.

As a pure science however, Comparative Religion is in the first instance an investigation into the facts of religious faith, into the religious beliefs, experiences and practices of mankind; and only in the second place is it concerned with their absolute truth, or the permanent reliability of the conceptions upon which they are based. Neither as a science is it called upon to pass judgement upon the relative superiority of the one form or system to the other. This will or may emerge in the course of the inquiry, but it is no part of the duty of the student of Comparative Religion to establish a scale of ascending or descending values. To be of any worth such a scale would have to be based upon general consent, and would be of little advantage if it represented merely the conviction of a portion of mankind. The Hindu or Buddhist, the Christian or Muhammadan, to say nothing of faiths less numerously attested and received, would frame his scale upon a basis and in a manner entirely different from that of his neighbour who professed another creed. He would not expect his estimate of comparative worth to be accepted by men of an alien faith. Perhaps the time may come when such a comparative estimate may be practicable and useful. Many would maintain that the time is appreciably nearer, and the problem more capable of solution than half a century ago. Meanwhile the student must possess his soul in patience, confident that in the final issue and judgement truth and right will prevail.

A further issue of much importance, not only historically but in view of the progress and development of the future, is opened up in the attempt to present an orderly arrangement or classification of religions. In what relation do they stand to one another, and in what terms may the answer to the problem of their historical connection be stated? By general consent the definitive distinction of true and false has been abandoned. It is at most relative; this or that religion contains a larger element of truth than another, and so far is justified in pressing its claims to acceptance upon men of an alien or different faith. None however is incapable of error, or speaks through its human instruments and advocates with infallible authority. The few hints or utterances that the sacred books of some religions give on this subject are not of much value. The Old Testament, for example, while it lays stress upon the unapproachable dignity and superiority of the Jewish faith, suggests that religious privilege and attainment have corresponded to ethnic divisions. Undoubtedly there is much truth underlying this conception, and history and experience have corroborated it to a very considerable extent. The analogy of physical relationship would point in the same direction. If the human race is one, of common origin but with many branches affiliated to the one stem, it would be reasonable to expect co-ordinate relationship between the various religious faiths of mankind, following in the main racial lines, and exhibiting the characteristics of the families of peoples by whom they have been conceived and elaborated. The problem is difficult; and Comparative Religion does not profess as yet to have co-ordinated all its elements, much less to be able to present a complete solution. Religion however has not been imposed from without, but save in exceptional circumstances developed from within. And this hypothesis of orderly development or evolution may be said to hold the field, and as it has been more fruitful than any other of verified and intelligible results, so it offers the most hopeful prospect of progress for the future.

Buddhism, for example, has established its position as the religion of the Mongolian and allied peoples. No other religious faith has found a response or welcome among them, or has been able to achieve any considerable proselytising success. If the suggestion should prove to be true, that the Śākya clan in which Gautama Buddha was born was of Scythian or Mongolian origin, it would be an interesting anticipation of the future history of the religion which he founded. Judaism and Muhammadism are Semitic faiths. The latter it is true has imposed itself to a considerable extent by force upon some non-Semitic peoples. But in the orthodox view the Aryan Persians are heretics; and the Chinese Muhammadans, except that they repeat the Muslim creed and listen to an Arabic Qur'ān that they do not understand, differ little in real belief from their Taoist or Confucian fellow-countrymen. The stronghold of Christianity has always been among the Aryan or Indo-European races. It has penetrated and won successes elsewhere, and has supported a claim to universality to a larger extent than any other faith. Its especial province nevertheless has been hitherto the Aryan, and especially the Latin and Anglo-Saxon peoples. Among these it has had no serious competitor, nor is any likely to arise.

Moreover a comparison of the results achieved and of the present position and prospects of religious belief in general justifies the assertion that of the leading faiths of the world Christianity alone contains the promise of the future. In the number of its adherents it is now in advance of any other religious system or confession, and as far as can be judged its numerical preponderance is rapidly increasing. Less striking, but perhaps more important and profound is the influence which its principles and ethical standards exert throughout the world, often in circles and amongst peoples not friendly to formal or doctrinal Christianity. This progress also has been made in spite of the fact that to a greater extent than probably any other religion the Christian presentation suffers from the divisions and inherited partisanship which are the legacy of a chequered history, and which hamper it in its endeavour to commend the truth which it holds to the non-Christian world. All religions that attempt to carry on an external propaganda are weakened more or less by similar disabilities and dissensions, which cripple from within its proselytising efforts abroad. Islām perhaps suffers least, its missionary work being almost entirely conducted by members of the orthodox and predominant sect. These internal divergences of faith and practice are themselves again parts of the conditions, the causes and extent of which the science of Comparative Religion sets itself to investigate; endeavouring to form a right estimate of their weight and importance as bearing upon the future as well as the past history of the faith, and affording some indication of the lines upon which creed and system may be expected to develop.

These considerations and a historical review of the evolution of religious systems do not lend support to a confident belief in a future synthesis or unification of the various faiths of the world. The tendency is in the direction of greater, not less specialisation of belief and thought. Neither in an investigation of the past nor in a just estimate of the conditions of the present is there ground for accepting unity of form or creed as a practicable ideal, a goal towards which effort may profitably direct itself; nor if it were attainable is there any reason to think that such a result would be to the advantage of mankind at large. Analogy at least would suggest what history confirms, that growth and movement are always towards diversity, and are not productive of uniformity or sameness. And if religious thought were an exception to the rule, the end would be deadness and decay, not spiritual life. The infinitely varied emotions and thoughts of mankind express themselves in infinitely varied forms and creeds; and it is impossible that the variety of belief should ever return to uniformity, or the likeness which characterises for instance the nature religions of primitive man. The ideal "unity of the faith" is a generous understanding and sympathy, which agreeing in the fundamental verities of belief and conviction is content to allow diversity in detail, and to be tolerant in all the lesser matters of creed and observance that belong rather to the fringe than to the centre and core of religious faith.

It would seem therefore impossible to forecast with any degree of confidence or certainty at so early a stage in the progress of the science the results to which the study of Comparative Religion may attain. It promises much, and the performance will not fall short of the promise. But the conclusions already reached and the fruits of the investigations that have been conducted do not suggest finality in any given system of religion as it exists at present or may be expected to develop in the near future. No known system is perfect, and on the practical side the science of Comparative Religion will aim rather at the elimination of that which is mistaken and false, and the conservation of all that is true, than at asserting or upholding the comparative superiority of one system or creed to another. Sufficient time and labour have been devoted in the past to attempts to demonstrate, often by violent methods, that this or that profession or faith possesses a monopoly of rightness and truth. The aim of Comparative Religion is rather by trial and comparison to make explicit and intelligible the varying relations of human beliefs in the religious sphere, to conserve that which is true and good and to dissipate error, and thus to conduct to a goal which if it appears ever to recede the more closely and definitely it is pursued is yet the noblest to which mankind can direct his efforts. The fruit however of all his efforts, so far as can be foreseen, will not be a closed system, inaccessible to new light and knowledge. There will be no final check or cessation in the ingathering of the fresh results of wisdom and research. The path to be trodden is marked by movement and growth, not by stagnation and decay. And if there is a limit to the assimilation of truth by the human mind and heart, or the growth of the moral and spiritual life, the end so conceived or imagined is hardly within the purview of a science which hopes all things and holds fast that which is good.

BIBLIOGRAPHY

It would be altogether impossible to present here a complete bibliography of a subject so vast in its scope and so far-ranging. A few of the more important works are mentioned, which the student will find to be interesting and suggestive for further reading. Very many are of necessity omitted, and further contributions are made almost every year to the number of publications which deal with the subject of Comparative Religion. All volumes are published in London, unless otherwise stated.

Introductory and General

A few books also are recorded here for their general value, though they have reference only to one phase or aspect of the subject. They are not however naturally included under the later headings of this bibliography.

Balfour, A. J., *Foundations of Belief*, 1901; *Theism and Humanism*, 1915.

Caird, E., *Evolution of Religion*, 2 vols., 1893.

Chantepie de la Saussaye, Ph.D., *Lehrburch der Religionsgeschichte*[3], 2 vols., Tübingen, 1905.

Clodd, E., *Animism*, in the series "Religions, Ancient and Modern," 1905. The remaining vols. of the series are special, of much though unequal value, and give brief useful conspectus of their respective subjects.

CRAWLEY, A. E., *Idea of the Soul*, 1909.

EUCKEN, R., *Hauptprobleme der Religionsphilosophie der Gegenwart*, Berlin, 1912.

FARNELL, L. R., *Evolution of Religion*, 1905.

FRAZER, J. G., *Belief in Immortality*, 1913; *Golden Bough*[3], 12 vols., 1907 ff., a most interesting and valuable collection of facts, material, and illustrative examples bearing upon early religion, belief and practice; the author's successive theories however have not met with universal acceptance, and are by no means to be considered as established; *Totemism and Exogamy*, 4 vols., 1910.

GALLOWAY, G., *Philosophy of Religion*, Edinburgh, 1914.

GEDEN, A. S., *Studies in the Religions of the East*, 1913.

GOULD, S. BARING, *Origin and Development of Religious Belief*, 2 vols., 1884.

GRANT, G. M., *Religions of the World*, new edition, 1895, and often reprinted.

HOWARD, E., *Studies of Non-Christian Religions*, 1907.

JEVONS, F. B., *Introduction to the History of Religion*[4], 1908.

JORDAN, L. H., *Comparative Religion, Its Adjuncts and Allies*, 1915.

LANG, A., *Myth Ritual and Religion*, 2 vols., new impression, 1906; *Making of Religion*[2], 1900; *Social Origins*, 1903; *Secret of the Totem*, 1905.

LUBBOCK, J., *Marriage Totemism and Religion*, 1911.

MARRETT, R. R., *Threshold of Religion*[2], 1914.

MARTINEAU, J., *Study of Religion*, 2 vols., 1889.

MCDOUGALL, W., *Body and Mind*, 1911, a full and capable defence of Animism.

MÜLLER, F. MAX, *Introduction to the Science of Religion*, new edition, 1893; *Lectures on the Origin and Growth of Religion*, new edition, 1891; *Gifford Lectures*, in 4 vols: *Natural, Physical, Anthropological and Psychological Religion*, 1891 to 1895.

RÉVILLE, A., *Prolegomena to the History of Religions*, 1884.
REINACH, S., *Cults Myths and Religions*, translated E. Frost, 1912.
SEELEY, J. R., *Natural Religion*, 1891.
SMITH, W. ROBERTSON, *Religion of the Semites*, new edition, 1894.
STRATTON, G. M., *Psychology of the Religious Life*, 1911.
TIELE, C. P., *Elements of the Science of Religion*, 2 vols., 1897 and 1899; *Outlines of the History of Religion*, 1892.
WESTERMARCK, E., *Origin and Development of the Moral Ideas*, 2 vols., 1906 and 1908.

HINDUISM

BARTH, A., *Religions of India*[3], 1891.
CROOKE, W., *Popular Religion and Folk-Lore of Northern India*, 2 vols., 1896.
DEUSSEN, P., *Religion and Philosophy of India, the Upanishads*, Eng. transl., Edinburgh, 1906; *Sechzig Upanishads der Veda*, Leipzig, 1897.
DUBOIS, J. A., *Hindu Manners, Customs, and Ceremonies*[3], Eng. transl., Oxford, 1906.
FRAZER, R. W., *Indian Thought, Past and Present*, 1915.
HAVELL, E. B., *Benares the Sacred City*, 1905.
HOPKINS, E. W., *Religions of India*, 1896.
MACNICOL, N., *Indian Theism*, Oxford, 1915.
MARTIN, O. O., *Gods of India*, 1914.
MONIER-WILLIAMS, M., *Brāhmanism and Hinduism*[4], 1891.
MÜLLER, F. MAX, *Six Systems of Indian Philosophy*, 1899.
OMAN, J. C., *Cults Customs and Superstitions of India*[2], 1908; *Mystics Ascetics and Saints of India*, 1903.
SCHOMERUS, H. W., *Der Śaiva Siddhānta*, Leipzig, 1912.

STEVENSON, SINCLAIR (MRS.), *Heart of Jainism*, Oxford, 1915; *Rites of the First Born*, *ib.*, 1920.

WESTCOTT, G. A., *Kabīr and the Kabīr Panth*, Cawnpore, 1907.

WHITEHEAD, H., *The Village Gods of South India*, Oxford, 1916.

WILKINS, W. J., *Modern Hinduism*, 1887; *Hindu Mythology, Vedic and Puranic*, Calcutta, 1882.

The Indian articles in J. Hastings' *Encyclopædia of Religion and Ethics*, Edinburgh, 1908 ff., are of especial interest and value.

BUDDHISM

BAYNES, H., *Way of the Buddha*, 1906.

BEAL, S., *Buddhism in China*, 1884.

COPLESTON, R. S., *Buddhism in Magadha and Ceylon*[2], 1908.

DAVIDS, C. A. F., *Buddhism, a Study of the Buddhist Norm*, 1912.

DAVIDS, T. W. RHYS, *Lectures on the Origin and Growth of Religion as illustrated by the History of Indian Buddhism*, 1881; *Buddhism*, new edition, 1910.

EDKINS, J., *Chinese Buddhism*[2], 1893.

GILES, H. A., *Confucianism and its Rivals*, 1915.

HACKMANN, H., *Buddhism as a Religion*, 1910.

HARDY, R. SPENCE, *Manual of Buddhism*[2], 1880.

JOHNSTON, R. F., *Buddhist China*, 1913.

KERN, H., *Manual of Indian Buddhism*, Strassburg, 1896.

LLOYD, A., *The Creed of Half Japan*, 1911.

MONIER-WILLIAMS, M., *Buddhism*, 1889, the most reliable and complete manual, unfortunately out of print.

NARASU, P. LAKSHMI, *Essence of Buddhism*[2], Madras, 1912.

NUKARIYA, KAITEN, *Religion of the Samurai*, 1913.

ROCKHILL, W. W., *Life of the Buddha*, 1884.

SAUNDERS, K. J., *Buddhist Ideals*, Madras, London and Colombo, 1912; *Story of Buddhism*, Oxford, 1916; *The Buddha's Way of Virtue*, 1912.
SHWAY YEO, *The Burman, His Life and Notions*[3], 1910.
SUZUKI, D. T., *Outlines of Mahāyāna Buddhism*, 1907.
T SDALL, W. St. C., *Noble Eight-Fold Path*, 1903.
WADDELL, L. A., *Buddhism of Tibet or Lamaism*, 1895.
WARREN, H. C., *Buddhism in Translations*, Cambridge, Massachusetts, 1896.

Reliable translations of the sacred books of the Hindu, Buddhist, and other religions will be found in the series of *Sacred Books of the East*, published by the Oxford University Press.

JUDAISM AND CHRISTIANITY

ABELSON, J., *Jewish Mysticism*, 1913.
FRIEDLANDER, M., *Text Book of the Jewish Religion*[4], 1896.
GLOVER, T. R., *The Jesus of History*, 1917.
GRAETZ, H. H., *History of the Jews*, transl. B. Löwy and others, 6 vols., Philadelphia, 1891–98.
Jewish Encyclopædia, ed. I. Singer, 12 vols., 1901 ff., a great and worthily conceived and written store of information on the history and religion of the Jews.
KENNEDY, H. A. A., *St. Paul and the Mystery Religions*, n.d. (1913).
KUENEN, A., *Religion of Israel to the Fall of the Jewish State*, 3 vols., 1874–75.
MONTEFIORE, C. G., *Lectures on the Origin and Growth of Religion as illustrated by the Religion of the Ancient Hebrews*, 1892; *Judaism and St. Paul*, 1914.
PETERS, J. P., *Religion of the Hebrews*, 1914.
RICHTER, J., *History of Missions in India*, transl. S. H. Moore, Edinburgh and London, 1908; *History of Missions in the Near East*, 1910.

ROBERTSON, J., *Early Religion of Israel*, 1892.

ROGERS, R. W., *Cuneiform Parallels to the Old Testament*, n.d. (1912).

SCHECHTER, S., *Some Aspects of Rabbinic Theology*, 1909; *Studies in Judaism*, two series, 1896 and 1908.

STANLEY, A. P., *Lectures on the History of the Jewish Church*, 3 vols., 1866–1877.

WELLHAUSEN, J., *Prolegomena to the History of Israel*, transl. J. S. Black and Allan Menzies, Edinburgh, 1885.

The most convenient and reliable Bible Dictionaries are those edited by J. Hastings, 5 vols., Edinburgh, 1898 to 1904; and the *International Standard Bible Encyclopædia*, also in 5 vols., edited by J. Orr and others, Chicago and London, 1915.

MUHAMMADANISM

AMEER ALI, SYED, *Spirit of Islam*, 1902.

ARNOLD, T. W., *Preaching of Islam*², 1913.

BROOMHALL, M., *Islam in China*, 1910.

HUGHES, T. P., *Dictionary of Islām*², 1896.

Islam and Missions, Lucknow Conference Report, 1911, London and New York, n.d.

MACDONALD, D. B., *Development of Muslim Theology, Jurisprudence, and Constitutional Theory*, 1903.

MARGOLIOUTH, D. S., *Early Development of Muhammadanism*, 1914; *Mohammed and the Rise of Islam*, 1905.

NICHOLSON, R. A., *Mystics of Islam*, 1914.

MUIR, W., *Caliphate*, 1899; *Life of Mahomet*³, 1894.

SELL, E., *Essays on Islām*, Madras and London, 1901; *Faith of Islam*,², 1896; *Historical Development of the Quran*, 1909; *Life of Muhammad*, London, Madras and Colombo, 1913.

SHEDD, W. A., *Islam and Oriental Churches*, Philadelphia, 1904.
STOBART, J. W. H., *Islam and its Founder*, 1877.
TISDALL, W. St. C., *Religion of the Crescent*, 1910.
WOLLASTON, A. N., *Muhammad his Life and Doctrines* 1904.

ADDENDA

HÖFFDING, H., *Philosophy of Religion*, Eng. transl., 1906.
OESTERLEY AND BOX, *Religion and Worship of the Synagogue*², London, 1911.
REISCHAUER, A. K., *Studies in Japanese Buddhism*, New York, 1917.
TUCKWELL, J. H., *Religion and Reality*, New York.

INDEX